PERFORMANCE

Anthony Rooley, lutenist, sculptor, writer and director of the *Consort of Musicke* has spent his life delving into and resurrecting the forgotten musical masterpieces of the Renaissance. But being very much a man of today, he is not content merely to present his finds in the scholarly manner of a musical archaeologist, but rather aims for an inspired communication to take place during the act of performance, involving performer, composer and hearers alike.

Rooley's *Consort of Musicke,* which he founded in 1969, has won the respect and love of audiences around the world, as has his duo combination with Emma Kirkby (sometimes extended to a trio with bass David Thomas or soprano Evelyn Tubb). As a sculptor, he continues his exploration into the meaning of performance by experimenting with the unexpected in wood, iron, and stone.

Performance

REVEALING THE
ORPHEUS WITHIN

Anthony Rooley

ELEMENT BOOKS

© Anthony Rooley 1990

First published in Great Britain in 1990 by
Element Books Limited
Longmead, Shaftesbury, Dorset

Cover illustration by Hanife Hassan O'Keeffe
Cover design by Max Fairbrother
Designed by Roger Lightfoot
Typeset by Footnote Graphics,
Warminster, Wiltshire
Printed and bound in Great Britain by
Billings, Hylton Road, Worcester

British Library Cataloguing in Publication Data
Rooley, Anthony, 1944–
Performance: revealing the Orpheus within.
1. Music. Performances, history
I. Title
781.43

ISBN 1–85230–160–0

Illustrations
'Performer and Audience'
Musikgeschichte in Bildem, W. Salmen, Vol III/9, Leipzig, 1976
'Songs of Mourning' title page
Facsimile of 1613 edition by Scolar Press, Menston, 1970
'Time Stands Still' incipit
Facsimile of 1603 edition by Scolar Press, Menston, 1970

Contents

Acknowledgements

The major part of this book was written at our family home in the Yorkshire Dales, with log-fire burning, dales view inspiring, and an atmosphere conducive to creative writing – an atmosphere maintained by Carla, and occasional light relief injected by Abigail, Rebekah and Hannah. All four listened to great tracts of emerging Orphic utterances, and gave suitable responses of delight or horror. For some reason I became known (for a short time only, thank goodness) as Sir Epicure Mammon – perhaps in response to the chapter which digresses into a culinary anecdote.

For twenty-one years I have worked in rehearsal and in performance with the members of the Consort of Musicke – a number of musicians of great stature have worked under this name for varying lengths of time. I have been fortunate to work closely with artists of great inspiration, and I have learned much about the art and craft of performance with these colleagues. I think particularly of Catherine Mackintosh, Trevor Jones, James Tyler and others from the earliest days; but also such as David Thomas, with whom I have kept a more constant link. However it is the singers who make up the vocal ensemble to whom I owe most. So many hours of preparation together, building a 'decoro' of great strength, so many extraordinary performances where 'sprezzatura' has abounded. Recent members like Joe Cornwell, Rufus Müller and Richard Wistreich I remember with great affection, but the present roll-call – Evelyn Tubb, Mary Nichols, Paul

Agnew, Andrew King and Alan Ewing have my deepest gratitude and admiration. Emma Kirkby, too, has been an essential
ingredient in this performing alchemy for many years, and
it is her artistry and presence on the platform which has
encouraged the development of some of the ideas contained in
this book. For many she epitomises 'the English Nightingale' of
our time – the bird directly inspired by Orpheus' song.

Holding this ensemble of singers together (and a director of
erratic waywardness) is no mean feat. Virginia Rounding,
our administrator, and my personal assistant, would deserve
great accolades if that was all she did. But in addition she
typed this entire book, making judicious changes in sentence
construction and spelling when necessary, and has always
devoted herself to the task even when she found the more
obscure philosophic flights of fancy went against the grain.
Virginia, thank you! Without your assistance this, and many
other projects besides, would have been impossible.

A number of colleagues apart from the Consort of Musicke
have been inspirational, directional or supportive for many
years. Particularly I would like to thank Wilfrid Mellers,
whose inspiration in lectures, in books and in his music is
already mythic. But it is himself, as a person, that makes me
regard him as a living, loving legend. Joscelyn Godwin, a
thinker and writer of such stature – I see him as a gentle giant
of ancient wisdom. It was he who first introduced me to the
'invisible college' which knows no barriers of geography or
time. Noel Cobb is another such person: I have just finished
reading his Foreword to Tom Moore's 'The Planets Within',
a study of the astrological psychology of Ficino, and it is
typical of Noel's intellectual and spiritual generosity to spur
others on so. Cherry Gilchrist was also generous in her urging
me to write this book – it was she who encouraged me to
start this undertaking, and now it is finished I can truly say I
am glad she did. Colleagues of a different sort I thank in a
different way: the Famiglia Carrara, with their chief inspiration for this generation, Titino Carrara. I can only say, and
this is meant to be a compliment, it was like working with the

denizens of an ancient forest – so primitive is their inspiration I began to believe, for the first time since I was nine, in the fauns, satyrs, dryads, naiads, Pan and Bacchus of our own archetypal undergrowth. Thank you, all of you in the Famiglia Carrara, for returning my faith to this pre-Christian world.

An inspiration of a different sort I have received from all the many people around the globe who have taken part in study programmes. In the normal world these participants are called 'students', but often they appear as 'masters'. The terms are interchangeable, but certainly I have learned at least as much from them, as they *think* they have from me. One very special group of about twenty-five people made up a team called 'Music in Focus' in 1976–7. If any of you read this work now, you alone will realise how much it is indebted to our inspirational soul-searching. Thank you all.

Now there are several people who, mostly unwittingly, contributed to moments of personal revelation. I hope they are not embarrassed to be mentioned here. First, when I was fifteen, there was a group of completely anonymous youths who formed a Morley skiffle group. Their music, their performance, carried the power to move me to follow this life's work. Next came the Wilkinson Family, once of East Ardsley, later of Norwich, who introduced me to Spanish Flamenco, and my first real guitar – a hand-made Wilkinson Flamenco guitar. Here I was introduced to the 'rasgueado' and 'duende' for the first time. A quite unwitting transmitter of revelation was, shortly after, the great harpsichordist of the fifties and sixties, George Malcolm. I have recently thanked him personally, and he was much amused to know he led me from Flamenco to Bach.

Finally there are a number of performers whose work has continued to reveal Orpheus to me. Forgive me, all of you, for reducing your mention to a list, but I can assure you this list is *potent*! The sarangi player, Ram Narayan – music direct from the Divine; Bobby McFerrin, the unique voice; Sarah Vaughan, untimely deceased genius of jazz with baroque ornamentation; Parween Sultana, perhaps the greatest vocalist of our generation; Frances Kelly, a harpist with the most delicate touch; Jeff Healey, true to blues, blind and yet seeing the light; Little Richard, the most handsome blues singer ever born he tells us, but his music carries real *power*. I have already mentioned the uncrowned Queen of Early Music, Emma Kirkby; next comes the great Flamenco artist, Terremoto; then our finest baroque lutenist, Nigel North. I must reiterate my admiration for David Thomas, who holds a stage and an audience like Orpheus incarnate. Then there are anonymous Bulgarian chanters living in the Shadow of the Mountain: Evelyn Tubb, who sings like someone reborn; the monks of Chevratoigne, continuing the ancient, orthodox spirit; David Hikes and his Harmonic Choir who are creating a new chant for a future world; and finally Richard Goode, who plays Beethoven just like it is being composed.

All these wonderful musicians, and many more besides that I still have to discover, tell me that Orpheus is alive and well and living inside each of us, if we have ears to hear and hearts to move.

Anthony Rooley
June 1990

For Euridice
in whatever guise she manifests.

Introduction

THE basic stories relating to Orpheus are well-known – they have been retold many times, analysed for their 'symbolic' content, raided by psychologists, psychiatrists and mystics, and are now retold as stories for children. Indeed Orpheus and his actions have almost become the stuff of fairy story and we, in our adult state of knowledge, hardly think of them in a literal sense. After all we cannot prove, through archaeology or any other means, that such a man ever actually lived. We have never found his lyre, either whole or in fragments, and there is no sign of the skull – all that we could expect to remain of the severed singing head.

But in other times thinkers have not been stopped from believing by the absence of evidence. Educated men and women of the Renaissance, for example, believed literally in myths and legends surrounding the figure of Orpheus. An educated and yet innocent view of such myths must be close to true knowledge – an almost child-like view which allows direct, powerful inspiration to play on an artist's work, a poet's words and a musician's notes.

Happily, we are not so far from this naive state of wonder and awe that we cannot for a few moments put aside our need for data, and be suddenly deeply moved by a piece of music, a particular line in a poem, or a familiar painting seen from a fresh angle. Performances of various kinds, in various arts, can stop us in our analytic tracks and send a shiver down the spine. We do not especially want to analyse such a feeling, partly because we're afraid the experience might be swamped by analytic techniques, and anyway all other departments of our experience are measured, weighed, proved, X-rayed – something, surely, should be left inviolate.

I am writing here precisely about the experience in the moment of performance. I do attempt to analyse the energies which are at play in performance, but I also try to show a synthesis which leaves these truly precious experiences intact. The whole exercise is to go deeper in, simply so that performance can fulfil its purpose more effectively.

For years the BBC in its wisdom deemed that for its Third Programme talks about music were infra dig. Music should speak for itself, therefore the anouncements would be minimal and delivered as fact only. There is, of course, some validity in this argument – an experience of fine music is so profound, potentially, that no amount of talking can add anything to that experience. But when the announcements begin to dry out, to lose any sense of excitement, to begin to sound stuffy and pompous, to be afraid to string a couple of adjectives together in case the experience might be coloured for others, then the music begins to be weighed down with inertia, and all sense of performance begins to founder. There are some gifted people, however, who really can talk about their art – Paul Klee wrote at length, Picasso gave a few rascally, inspiring interviews, Humph Lyttelton seems rarely to be lost for words. The spirit of creativity can spill over into our ordinary language, so that suddenly there is a performance in another medium. Actually it is not about *what* you say, it is *how* you say it – if it carries inspiration, enthusiasm, wit and energy then it has a touch of Orpheus in it. We can expand our awareness of what allows that special tingling sensation to occur.

I want to define the word 'performance' as I am using it here. I am expressing a philosophical view which understands that from birth to death, our entire 70-year span (or whatever is our allotted length) is nothing, but nothing, other than a play, a performance. Each of us plays a part, or a series of parts, more or less willingly, more or less consciously, more or less capably. Every action, interplay of relationships, pursuits of all kinds can be seen as 'performance'. At times it seems as though such a view may take all spontaneity out of everything, only for us to discover that potentially it leads to yet greater freedom. If we play our roles with ease, unselfconsciously, with love and care, then through our play we may blossom, and those around us too.

Those arts which are known as 'the performing arts' have a very particular function in our artistic/social/spiritual experiences. They offer, I believe, in the moment of performance, a ritual which has relevance for our entire lives, if we choose to see it that way. The experience of performance contains such powerful things: heightened states of awareness, time seeming to stand still, moments of incredible clarity, moments of beautiful reverie, a sense of wonder, awesome beauty and love, profound admiration and respect. These brief, intense moments become magnified in an artistic ritual experience which is out of the ordinary. But all these delights are also to be found in the ordinary – if only we will let the natural thing happen, and not block it with negativity, boredom, habit and other abuses.

Official 'performances' exist, one could say, to act as a reminder or as a salutary shot in the arm to pull us out of our daily dullness and remind us a little of how intensely rich human experience can be. Every action can, I believe, be imbued with a sense of wonder: it may be a revelation to chop a cabbage, to exchange ideas in fine conversation, to take a walk, to breathe fresh air, to go to the loo, to dress, to sleep and rise, to move in a childlike state of grace from birth to death. That is the potential – but we forget, we fail, we fall – we are, after all, only human. But ritual performance can strengthen and remind and recharge us. Orpheus is really the archetypal performer, receiving his inspiration directly from the Divine, and through this gift, giving it out to all those with ears to hear. Orpheus should really be every performer's pagan patron saint, for we cannot do better than follow his example. Except perhaps we can stop for a moment and realise, with Jung and his school of thought, that the archetypal image or symbol has power precisely because we carry it imprinted in us in some way. The Orpheus within can be nursed and nurtured so that *our very own song* can begin to be sung, so that our brief play may become more tuneful, and delight in its own re-sounding.

CHAPTER ONE

The concept of 'performance'
in the sixteenth century

L IKE everything else, attitudes to performance have gone through endless changes over the last few hundred years – in Western culture alone, quite aside from the exotic differences in other cultures. The functions of the composer and performer, and the nature of the audience are constantly shifting. Habit, custom, and the unquestioning adoption of the 'received tradition' lead us into very distorted views of how our forebears understood performance. In fact, Europe of the sixteenth century is as far removed from our own frame of thought as is, say, ancient Chinese civilisation. Warning lights should go on if it suddenly seems too close and comfortable, for behind apparently familiar words lie whole modes of thought that transform the understanding.[1]

As a simple example, take the word 'artificial'. Today we imply a slur if something is thought to be artificial. It is in some way second-class. Yet one great composer from Italy working in England was described in print in 1610 as 'the most artificial and famous Alfonso Ferrabosco of Bologna'.[2] Clearly the writer was intending the highest of praise, without reserve. The word has virtually reversed its meaning from being 'full of deep skill and art' to 'shallow, contrived and almost worthless'. Now this switch, in 400 years, in what purports to be the same language, suggests we should be wary of *anything* that appears familiar – it may have meant for the minds of the time something quite other.

What did 'performance' mean for sixteenth century European culture? Only a complex answer will do in reply, for society worked on several levels, and different times and places imposed different demands on the performers. These performers ranged from travelling vagabonds with minimal musical skill, through the town and city waits who served the community, to amateurs who devoted their spare energy after their work as merchants, on to professional musicians employed by wealthy households, the church or the court, and eventually to the courtier himself cultivating a skill on the lute, viol or keyboard as part of his gentlemanly accomplishments.[3] Perhaps the final level of accomplishment was to be found in the few virtuosi who travelled Europe finding a welcome wherever their name had gone before – performers who sometimes commanded, we are told, as high a salary as the Admiral of the Fleet.[4] I want to look at this last, elevated level of performance, for it appears to be closest to our 'star system' created by the power of modern media. On inspection, though, the differences are far greater than the similarities.

Only tantalisingly brief glimpses can be had from the sixteenth century of those virtuosi who were praised to the skies. I take a picture, an account, and emblematic encomium to present my case, then look to self-improvement manuals of the time which refer to music in the course of a search for techniques which lead to experiences of ennoblement. From these we discern three main principles, or attitudes which can channel the energies of the performer.

MARSILIO FICINO

Let us begin with a woodcut, made at the court of the Medici in Florence in the 1490s, and intended to illustrate the power of inspired performance.[5]

This woodcut probably depicts an occasion at the country villa at Carreggi, where the Medici court retired to enjoy the platonic discourses of the great teacher Marsilio Ficino. It

may even be him playing the lyra-da-braccio, for we know from his writings that he regularly exercised himself in singing the hymns of Orpheus to the accompaniment of the lyra – for his own and his followers' edification. He dwells at length on the benefits of 'drawing down' stellar influences, and describes in detail the ways this can best be achieved. For example

> Our spirit is consonant with the heavenly rays which, occult or manifest, penetrate everything. We can make it still more consonant if we vehemently direct our affections towards the star from which we wish to receive a certain benefit . . . above all, if we apply the song and light suitable to the astral deity and also the odour, as in the hymns of Orpheus.[6]

The gathering is about the size Ficino thought best for profound study, and the auditor nearest to us is clearly quite carried away, with his limbs cast in careless deportment, bereft of his senses for the time being. The rest are thoroughly attentive, attention transfixed. In some paintings of Orpheus, from the early years of the sixteenth century, we are shown rays of light entering his up-turned eyes, from heaven.

FRANCESCO DA MILANO

Now we turn to a beautiful description of an improvised performance by the famed lutenist Francesco da Milano, known as 'Il Divino'. This is a rare eyewitness account, unique from this time (before 1546 when Francesco died):

> While staying in Milan ... Jacques Descartes was invited to a sumptuous and magnificent banquet ... where, among other pleasures of rare things assembled for the happiness of those select people, appeared Francesco da Milano – a man who is considered to have attained the end (if such is possible) of perfection in playing the lute well. The tables being cleared, he chose one, and as if tuning his strings, sat on the end of a table seeking out a fantasia. He had barely disturbed the air with three strummed chords when he interrupted conversation which had started among the guests. Having constrained them to face him, he continued with such a ravishing skill that little by little, making the strings languish under his fingers in his sublime way, he transported all those who were listening into so pleasurable a melancholy that – one leaning his head on his hand supported by his elbow, and another sprawling with his limbs in careless deportment, with gaping mouth and more than half-closed eyes, glued (one would judge) to those strings (of the instrument), and his chin fallen on his breast, concealing his countenance with the saddest taciturnity ever seen – they remained deprived of all senses save that of hearing, as if the spirit, having abandoned all the seats of the senses had retired to the ears in order to enjoy the more at its ease so ravishing a harmony; and I believe (said M. de Ventimille) that we would be there still, had he not himself – I know not how – changing his style of playing with a gentle force, returned the spirit and the senses to the place from which he had stolen them, not without leaving as much astonishment in each of us as if he had been elevated by an ecstatic transport of some divine frenzy.[7]

This account is well-known by the specialist fraternity of late twentieth century lutenists, and has been raided for any fragments of information on luteplaying styles and techniques, but the profound insights it offers on attitudes to performance have largely been ignored. It actually tells us so much. Francesco's improvisations were controlled and directed by him to ravish, deliberately, the senses of his listeners. In fact the description of one whose eyes were glued to the strings reminds us of some in the front row listening to the lyra-dabraccio player. Even more striking is the listener whose body is carelessly awry, exactly like our man with his head in his hands. Actually I think both woodcut and account are depicting the same basic notion – a fine musical performance can lift the soul right out of the listener's body for a short while – a concept to which we will return in a moment.

The grand title given to Francesco of 'Il Divino' needs looking at a little more closely.[8] Michelangelo was also known as an 'Il Divino',[9] and John Dowland, around 1600 was known as 'the English Orpheus'.[10] Even a century later Purcell was dubbed the 'Orpheus Britannicus'.[11] What do these extravagant titles mean other than that the recipients were deeply admired? Simply put, it was recognised by men of their own age that these performers carried the fabled power of Orpheus to move the soul, they were able through their art to communicate, fairly directly, the divine inspiration which had been symbolically granted to Orpheus. Movements of the soul in the body are rather dimly perceived in our time, we are a touch embarrassed by the language and vocabulary needed for such a 'subjective' thing, and dismiss such talk as over-poetic. Shakespeare had no such qualms as he made Lorenzo explain to Jessica the reason why we cannot partake in the awesome music of the spheres:

> But, whilst this muddy vesture of decay [the body]
> Doth grossly close it [the soul] in, we cannot hear it
> [the music of the spheres].[12]

The true task of the performer is that of 'soul-tickling' –

drawing the soul, via the means of the aural sense, out of the body, through the aperture of the ears, as though it were extended on subtle stalks. A slightly odd image perhaps, but one which serves to illustrate the vast Renaissance literature on the need to unseat the soul trapped in the 'muddy vesture of decay' because otherwise the soul becomes locked in, and forgets its true home (partaking of divine essence, rather than gross substance). The literature stresses that the senses can trap us into further misery, or can act as 'windows' for the soul to peep out and see beyond the physical universe. There is the tale of the platonic kiss, the souls come to the lips, meet, delight, exchange and inhabit the other's body. Then, when parted, the lovers' anguished longing is in fact the two souls bereft, and they are not assuaged until meeting and kissing again! How simple and enticing, and what a beautiful union of body and soul is implied by the story.

COURTLY LOVE

The story of the kiss is told by the Italian platonic poet Pietro Bembo in Baldassare Castiglione's book 'Il Cortegiano' [1528],[13] along with an amazing body of other lore relating to the life of the courtier and his lady. The prose style is somewhat dense for modern readers, but perseverance pays. Essentially what is outlined by Castiglione is the exact nature of court life, why it is of fundamental importance, what are the right attitudes and practices to be encouraged, the responsibility each individual has to act in a seemly and ennobling manner. Here is the ultimate document for the concept of human life as a series of plays, with each courtier and lady being central actors.

In its own time it was seen as being of central significance. First published in Italian in Italy in the 1520s, it found a wide readership not only in the courtly circles, but also in the rising middle classes who wanted to imitate their social superiors. Self-improvement was the order of the day. The 'Book of the Courtier' was translated into most local languages, into

English by Sir Thomas Hoby in 1561, and studied avidly across Europe. Apart from the Bible, no other book had such influence in the sixteenth century. It was imitated by other writers of socially improving manuals, and in England Henry Peacham finally closed an era with his 'The Compleat Gentleman' [1622], which is a reworking and an updating of Castiglione's ideas.[14] And so, for over 100 years, these improvement manuals held sway, stuffed full of valuable information on performance, both in the general 'all the world's a stage' sense, and specifically, since references to music abound.

From this central body of material then, the following insights are drawn. Here is a philosophy of performance as refreshing and relevant now as it was when first penned by Castiglione at the beginning of the sixteenth century. Three principles emerge: the first is that of *decoro*, the outward show, the appearance of things, all that which the assiduous student (of life or of the performing arts) can control and study, develop and refine. Included here is a sense of duty and dedication, a care in preparation and an ever-refining sense of what is appropriate. All things related to practice and technique come under this heading. Finally *decoro* embodies all that is understood by tradition, the laws or rules which hold right conduct in place.[15]

Imagine, though, how stultifying life would be if *decoro* were the only principle by which we conducted ourselves. An over use of *decoro* leads inevitably to rigidity, to dullness, to a shallow 'empty decorum' lacking any inner spirit or strength. Yet much of our teaching system is based on this principle alone. Some may even be reading this and saying, 'What else is there?'

Fortunately, Castiglione does not let us down. The balancing principle to *decoro* is *sprezzatura* – a lightning-like energy which carries courage, boldness, even rashness, and excitement. The Englishman, Hoby, translated *sprezzatura* as a 'noble negligence'. It is a quality which cannot be practised (that would turn it back into the realm of *decoro*), yet experience, the greatest teacher, may help us to learn to deal with this fiery concept. *Sprezzatura* is a delighting in the moment, a love of improvisation, a kind of calculated care-lessness.[16] It is constantly fresh and responsive to changing moods, it is a sort of buffoonery that has wisdom. If it is such a good thing, then who needs *decoro*? But Hoby's translation of 'a noble negligence' is exactly right. *Sprezzatura* alone would eventually lead to ill discipline, messiness, mere negli-gence, but if we balance both *decoro* and *sprezzatura* together we have a pair of forces of unparalleled power, in terms of human conduct and awareness.

Consider the truth of our situation: we have no idea what is going to face us next in life, and traditionally, habitually, we face the unknown with a whole body of expectations, considerations, conditioned reflexes, etc. We assume the unexpected will not happen because it is more secure and familiar that way. *Decoro* rules and hems us in. Perhaps we can get away with that for much of our lives, but not if we wish to succeed as a performer. A performance given under such conditions stirs no one, the audience will not be moved (except to empty their seats at the first opportunity). So often we hear performances of this kind – technically excellent, even perfect – yet which do not touch us at all. I have been more deeply moved by a child with virtually no *decoro* who has delivered an imperfect performance of the moment. *Sprezzatura*, the ability to embrace the unknown *and enjoy it*, gives us a performance long to remember. Ritualised per-formances – in the concert hall, the theatre, the piazza, wherever – channel our awareness *because* they are ritualis-tic, but what we perceive there can illumine our daily lives, our myriad of 'small' performances. Indeed if they do not, then they are little more than a diversion, a pleasant escape. The choice is ours of course.

If it were all so simple to achieve a balance between *decoro* and *sprezzatura*, we would be in a good way – for these are things we can grasp, or even make our own. But the pages of *The Courtier* are filled with a third, and utterly fundamental, principle to which *decoro* and *sprezzatura* bow down in submission. This central principle is *grazia*.

Grazia is not quite the same as the Christian concept of Grace – it is that, but with a touch of pagan magic about it as well. It is a quality from the Divine, uncontainable, unownable, without limit, belonging to no one; it will not manifest itself on request, but may, or may not, be present in any particular situation (or performance). Its presence is instantly recognised, by believer and unbeliever alike (though both will find different words to express it). Perhaps *grazia* is noticed first in the spaces between the notes, in the silences rather than the sounds. Some composers seem more able than others to aid its manifestation, yet they would be the first to acknowledge that it is not of their making; Josquin, Monteverdi, Bach, Mozart is the sort of roll-call that comes to mind. But it is in the performance rather than in the composition that *grazia* may descend.[17]

This first thing to learn of *grazia* according to Castiglione is that it is a gift, belonging to no one but its source of emanation. Ficino regarded it as 'divine frenzy', and yet also 'sublime tranquillity'. It is, writers agree, a state of bliss.

PERFORMANCE

Can the performing arts lay any claim to such high and mighty experiences? Well, no – because *grazia* cannot be claimed, but there is no doubt that certain performances may be a channel for this rarest of human experiences. An 'Il Divino' is so called because his or her art channels *grazia*. 'An ecstatic transport of divine frenzy' is how the listener described the experience of listening to Francesco da Milano's playing. A letter of Ficino describes more fully this divine frenzy and how it works on our souls:

> The soul receives the sweetest harmonies and numbers through the ears, and by these echoes is reminded and aroused to the divine music which may be heard by the more subtle and

penetrating sense of mind. According to the followers of Plato, divine music is twofold. One kind, they say, exists entirely in the eternal mind of God. The second is in the motions and order of the heavens, by which the heavenly spheres and their orbits make a marvellous harmony. In both of these our soul took part before it was imprisoned in our bodies. But it uses the ears as messengers, as though they were chinks in this darkness. By the ears, as I have already said, the soul receives the echoes of that incomparable music, by which it is led back to the deep and silent memory of the harmony which it previously enjoyed. The whole soul then kindles with desire to fly back to its rightful home, so that it may enjoy that true music again.[18]

Some readers may feel that in quoting Ficino the philosopher I am moving towards the over-exotic, away from the common world of awareness towards the mystic. The first point to make here is that Ficino's influence throughout the sixteenth century and much of the seventeenth was extraordinarily pervasive, and many of the things which he first clarified and stated with conviction later became accepted philosophy.[19] The second point is best embodied in two quotations, from men of the practical world, two composers from England – John Dowland writing in 1597, and Robert Jones in 1605. Their prefaces to books of songs are encomia to their respective patrons, and the content outlines the lineage of divine frenzy: Orpheus, Plato, Ficino (not mentioned by name, but quoted all the same) and the present writer. First Dowland, addressed to Sir George Carey, the Queen's Lord Chamberlain:

That harmony (Right honorable) which is skillfullie exprest by Instruments, albeit, by reason of the variety of number and proportion of it selfe, it easilie stirs up the minds of the hearers to admiration and delight, yet for higher authoritie and power hath been ever worthily attributed to that kinde of Musicke, which to the sweetnes of instrument applies the lively voice of man, expressing some worthy sentence or excellent Poeme. Hence (as al antiquitie can witnesse) first grew the heavenly Art of musicke: for Linus, Orpheus and the rest, according to the number and time of their Poemes, first framed the numbers and times of musicke: So that Plato defines melody to consist of harmony, number the common friend and uniter of them both. This small booke containing the consent of speaking harmony, joyned with the most musicall instrument the Lute, being my first labour, I have presumed to dedicate to your Lordship, who for your vertue and nobility are best able to protect it, and for your honourable favors towards me, best deserving my duety and service. Besides your noble inclination and love to all good Artes, and namely the divine science of musicke, doth challenge the patronage of all learning, then which no greater title can bee added to Nobilitie.[20]

Finally, from the pen of the prolific Robert Jones, a dedication to 'The Great Joy and Hope of Present and Future Times, Henrie, Prince of Wales' (he was to die in 1612 at the age of 18, so this joyful dedication became sadly ironic):

Almost all our knowledge is drawne through the senses, they are the Soules Intelligencers, whereby she passeth into the world, and the world into her, and amongst all of them, there is none so learned, as the eare, none hath obtained so excellent an Art, so delicate, so abstruse, so spirituall, that it catcheth up wilde soundes in the Aire, and bringes them under a governement not to be expressed, but done, and done by no skill but it owne. There is Musicke in all thinges, but every man cannot finde it out, because of his owne jarring, hee must have a harmony in himselfe, that shold goe about it, and then he is in a good way, as he that hath a good eare, is in a good forwardnes to our facultie. Conceite is but a well tunde fancy, done in time and place. An excellent sentence, is but a well tunde reason well knit together, Politie or the subject thereof, a Common wealth, is but a well tunde Song where all partes doe agree, and meete together, with full consent and harmony one serving other, and every one themselves in the same labour. But now I intrude into your Art, in which all pray (and see hopes) that God will give you a godly and prosperous knowledge, and then all other Artes shal prosper under it.[21]

In conclusion then, the Renaissance attitudes to the performing arts were that at best they could act as a direct channel of 'divine frenzy', carrying an Orphic power invested in the attuned performer, but capable of being emulated by the courtier, his lady, and later the merchant classes who sought to improve themselves. Life, as a performance, could be enhanced by *decoro*, *sprezzatura*, and *grazia*, and the most direct communication with the soul was through the 'windows', namely the senses, via the arts which appealed to different sensual appetites. The unseated soul could enjoy a sublime reverie and recall its rightful home, with the Divine. It appears to me that allowing for a rather more poetic language than is common today, these attitudes and principles are equally relevant now.

CHAPTER TWO

Some contemporary
thoughts on the art

IT is all very well for the remote, long-dead sixteenth century to have elaborate ideas and profound philosophy relating to performance, but what about now, the living present? What value can these arcane studies have for us?

Well it is perfectly obvious that I believe these ideas have tremendous value, they actually have much that is timeless about them, and therefore, do not date at all. Only terminology may prove a temporary barrier. In this chapter I want to present ideas in the form of two contrasting diagrams which show a formal performance situation, first, how it normally is, and secondly, how it might be with a simple shift of emphasis. Then we play some games with simple hierarchies and see how the role of artist/performer can be redefined.

First though, a personal tale, a shaggy dog story which highlights a common problem of weakness in a performing situation which will be readily familiar to most readers. I studied at the Royal Academy of Music in London in the early 1960s, as a classical guitarist – actually the first to go there and complete the three year LRAM (performers course) on classical guitar. I was regarded as an interesting experiment – hardly a serious music student at all. I didn't fit in the orchestra, nor the choir, I couldn't do keyboard harmony, my aural training was poor. Nor could I converse with other radiant and ardent students about Chopin, Liszt or Mahler, or the sonata form, or about 6/4, 5/3 chords, etc. I was, actually, a misfit. So I spent most of my second year studying archives on lute music in the British Library and began transcribing some of this priceless repertoire from obscure notation to guitar. The months ticked by, and suddenly it was time to present my plans for the final Recital Diploma – something no guitarist had ever done before me.

In good moments I was fairly confident I would knock the examiners sideways – after all I was working in an obscure area that few of them would know anything about – I had a fair amount of novelty value. So in a moment of excessive bravura, I planned a recital to finish all recitals – the most difficult pieces in the repertoire, many of which I had transcribed myself. Difficult fantasias, impressive fugues, and fingerbreaking suites of dances. I committed my plans to paper and sent it in. Once submitted, there was no going back. The nineteenth century rules ran, there was no adjusting. I broke into a cold sweat, and realised that the examination was only three months away.

Now a genuine *cold* sweat is quite rare, though most of us have had a touch of it and remember the experience for the rest of our lives. The palms of the hands perspire, the back of the neck parts company with the hairline, and there is a cold line of perspiration. At the base of the spine, just above the buttocks there is a shallow dimple which seems to become a reservoir of cold moisture. Everything in you seems to shrink and wants to hibernate. This is how I felt when I had handed in my recital programme. The pit of the stomach churned a bit too, but nothing compared to what I was to put it through during the next three months.

After a few hours I recovered my usual aplomb and again began to think how clever I had been in planning such a bold recital and soon I had fantasies even of playing like a master. I then experienced a glow, comforting, warm and very delightful.

In the next few weeks I oscillated between one experience and the other with increasing rapidity, and increasing extremeness. Unfortunately the cold began to outweigh the warm, I was on a downward spiral. Each day was passed with immense overweaning care. I did not know the word *decoro* but I was practising it with studious fidelity, and my self-imposed regime was unbelievable – up at 6, 1 hour slow scales, 1 hour difficult sections slowly, breakfast, 1 hour complete pieces slowly, 1 hour fast scales, 1 hour pieces at full speed. Each evening my patient wife had to listen to the complete recital, flaws and all, and any criticism from her, however mild, and we were almost to blows. My psychological constitution was delicate, to say the least.

As each day went by and my thoughts chanced to stray to the looming examination increasingly I became a stranger to myself. Thoughts would circle faster and faster, mistakes would start to happen where previously there were no difficulties, the programme seemed impossible, I smoked more, slept less and dreamed frequently of the day that was imminent.

Two days to go, and I woke from a nightmare where the examiners kept saying 'play louder, we cannot hear you'. I climbed out of bed and tumbled, not knowing which foot or leg was which. My ears had become so soured with over-straining to improve I found I could not even tune the instrument – there was no such thing any more as a pure interval. I was now a total stranger to myself, to my wife, to my instrument and to the music I had loved so much, and most of all to the examination I had to excel in. No forty-eight hours have ever hung so heavy, not even waiting for one of our babies to be born. And I had created this extreme, dramatic, pathetic turmoil myself. I was the only architect of the nightmare I was living.

Come the few moments before the examination and it hardly bears telling. In the back room there were several other hapless examinees, a mixed bag of cellists, pianists, flautists. At the doorway was a large can on the floor, placed thoughtfully should anyone feel uncontrollable nausea, and of course someone had, so that the smell invited one to undergo the same luckless experience. A bell rang, and my name was called and I found my legs propelling me on to the platform. One hand held the guitar by its slim neck but was perspiring so heavily I could hardly grip the thing and it threatened to slip out of my hand. My knees were weak and with each step I thought one would give way. My throat was unnaturally dry and my eyes were blurred. I could, however, see a table in the mid-distance of the large auditorium, covered in a green cloth on which was an old schoolstyle bell in brass, a jug of water with glasses, papers, and around the table five podgy faces that looked self-satisfied and seemed to say 'We've been through it in our time, and came through it with flying colours. The young ones are not made of the same stuff – show us, lad, if you dare'.

Now how one's mind can take in all that information, and fantasise on it in a distance of less than twelve paces is really quite astonishing and perhaps gives us hope for a different way of relating to this artificial, horrendous torture which I was going through. As I sat on the chair, I realised to my chagrin that my left knee had developed an uncontrollable wobble and as I placed the instrument on that thigh I realised things were not quite right. Add to that my right hand (used for plucking the strings) developed a shake which seemed to go the opposite way of the knee. The guitar was between the two dithering extremities, and I had to play it! Never have I felt less like a performer. I wanted the earth to swallow me up, I would rather have died than play a single note, and yet I had to play half-an-hour of some of the most difficult music for the instrument – *all chosen by me*!

As it turned out, once the fingers met the strings, I became absorbed by the music, and all fear, perspiration and shaking dropped away. I was given a pass with distinction and became the first classical guitarist to gain the LRAM and was invited to present a recital for the much coveted 'Recital Diploma'. So the whole thing began again. But this time I had experience on my side, I knew how good I was, I knew I was in a unique position and that my situation was unassailable. My ego felt well-fed from the recent trials and I was a master, perhaps a little young, but a master nonetheless. And so I planned an even more cunning programme – one with some profound intellectual message as well. I had something to say which everyone could learn from. I was, putting it mildly, rather special. Well of course this position of 'strength', just like the earlier position of 'weakness' wasn't constant. I occasionally had my doubts about this new recital programme, but I quickly reminded myself of the recent triumphs. But as the day for this second presentation came around (to which the press and agents were invited) I began to realise that I had bitten off more than I could chew. The bitter taste of foolhardy arrogance was in my mouth, but it had to be ignored, I had to see it through, somehow. Well I began by apologising that I wouldn't be playing exactly what was on their programmes, that some pieces hadn't been fully re-searched yet, but I hoped everyone would enjoy it. (Round of supportive applause!) Off I went, until the first memory lapse, so I started again, until the second memory lapse. So the evening continued, which existed, I am now sure, only for me to learn a simple lesson. False confidence, bloated ego and arrogance might fool other people for a while, but it never fools oneself. False humility, hiding your light, pretending you are worse than you are does not help anyone either. And the two extremes add up to the same thing – a totally false picture, which is an extremely common one for music-making today. In fact, it's the norm. Diagrammatically it looks like figure 1 (see p. 22).

I will just explain the parts of the diagram of conflict:

The *audience* as a body looks to where they rightly consider the action is to be, they are relatively passive, somewhat herdlike, but expecting to be entertained. The arrow from the outer circle in represents the direction of attention or energy flow. They see either a dominant performer (perhaps with skill, but certainly with a developed ego), or a weakling who feels incapable of occupying the hotseat. Either way they are either amazed, amused or embarrassed.

The *performer* considers himself to be at the centre, that he

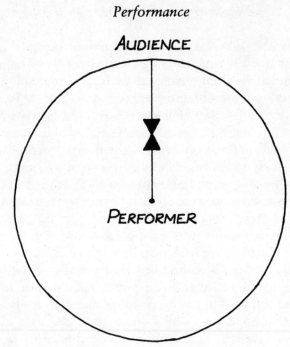

Figure 1

is the prime mover of the performance where he judges himself to be superior, adequate, or inferior to the auditors. His attention is, via his instrument and music, out to the audience, except for the energy absorbed by being the creator of the performance. The two forces of energy meet head on and lead to the following kinds of experience, depending on the performer's view of himself, and to a lesser extent on other factors, such as audience, acoustics, time, and place:

(1) the performer is an established 'name' in the media galaxy of stars and he/she can play superbly or rather badly, but the gloss of media hype hides the true quality of the performance

(2) the performer is on the lower echelons of the media star system, but is determined to advance, bludgeoning forward with a reinforced personality and ego, strong enough to take any knocks

(3) the performer is technically sound, sometimes better than in (1) or (2), but has not learned the need for personality projections, and is in effect a non-event, quickly forgotten by the audience

(4) the performer deems himself to be not really adequate for the situation, and is covered in embarrassment, apology and tentativeness. The audience might feel for the poor, abject individual (especially if they are blood relations) because they can easily identify themselves in that situation and are filled with horror at the thought. Nevertheless, it is a performance which, if it lives in the memory at all, is painful to recall

(5) the performer is bad, but is not sufficiently observant to have noticed this. He has a cast-iron ego and continues in spite of all outside messages to desist. Some performances of this kind are remembered only for their potential as after-dinner jokes.

All these types of performance fit on this first figure, which really is hardly satisfactory, yet is so widely prevalent. Sometimes, by who knows what power, perhaps the quality of the music itself, perhaps a certain 'something' in the atmosphere, a performance in this mould can suddenly transform into a deeply moving, seraphic or in some way profound experience – another dimension is traversed. This, however, is in spite of, rather than because of, any sound philosophy of performance, it is an accident that lifts the experience out of the mechanistic into the mystic.

There is another way of looking at the performing situation as a simple shift of emphasis which can transform the experience for everyone, performer and audience alike. It may at first seem like a diagrammatic or semantic trick, but it can yield results almost instantaneously, though the concept benefits from practice and experience. I have been applying this principle for twenty years and find it needs constant overhauling, constant fresh effort to bring it to the forward part of the mind. But I am absolutely certain this one simple concept has transformed my experience of performance, has been a positive aid to developing a successful career, and I have seen it have immediate good effect on groups of students throughout the world, allowing them to drop the fears and anxiety which I described with my RAM experience. Nervousness before a concert is normal, and to be expected, but the choice is to use that nervous energy to aid, or to mar your performing potential. Figure 1 almost always mars your performance, figure 2, however, can allow you to transcend your potential. This is it, in its simplicity:

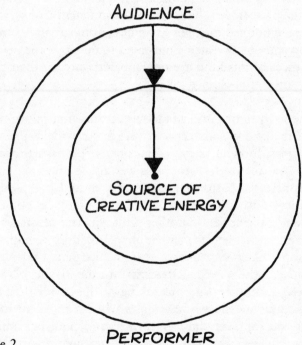

Figure 2

The diagram speaks for itself, but it is worth going through it step by step. The *audience* remains the same, they have little choice once they are in their seats. But it is worth noting that 95 per cent of an audience are there *because they want an enjoyable time*. They want an experience which they can cherish and will uplift them, though they would each use different words to describe why they are there. The other 5 per cent are made up of 'don't knows', and one or two of these are always people who harbour some jealousy, are carping critics, or in some way would not mind if the event wasn't much of a success. It is only a small percentage, but it is worth the performer acknowledging, as a positive point of recognition, that there *will* be a handful of Jeremiahs.

The *performer* now practises a different observation point. He or she strengthens the idea that the performer is not the centre or creator of the activity, but is responding to and transmitting a force of creative energy and inspiration which is *not of their making*. The famous spiritual simile of the individual being like an empty vessel, in order to resound God's praises more wholly, or to be filled with His ineffable Grace more completely is entirely appropriate here. This diagram helps the performer to empty himself, to let go of his own petty restrictions. To cease to think we are entirely responsible and the prime mover is a great relief. We become at once more able to respond, to be a better servant. We can more adequately per-form. By hyphenating the word in this way I am suggesting a subtle meaning of the word which is lost in common parlance. The implication is, I think, that the true task of the per-former is to bring into our sensual world those things (powers, energy, inspiration) which already exist in an un-formed stage – literally to 'bring into form'. The performer is then seen as a porter, a carrier, a transmitter, dipping into the subtle non-formed world and manifesting it in the tangible world of form. Commonly then, we accept the forms and grant the composer or performer (often one and the same in earlier times) with having created the form, when in fact they have only been messengers. In this common usage we do a grave disservice: to the performer; to ourselves; to the art; and ignore the source of creative inspiration.

In the second diagram this new centre point represents the

reservoir or sea of creativity. In mystical writers this great body of inspiration is unfathomable, unknowable, inexhaustible. The performer simply 'dips into' this great reservoir and brings back sustenance for all those with ears to hear (or eyes to see, depending which art form is under consideration). The task of the performer is now on quite a different plane from when the first diagram is in operation: it is marked by a flood of energy; by being refreshed by the performance rather than being exhausted by it. We can use the simile of the prism for the performer – the source of white light passes through the prism and presents a myriad of beautiful colours for the beholder on the further side, such colours as give rise to reverie and inspiration, so that the beholder looks to the prism to see the source of wonder beyond it.

Now in this diagram the performer takes the audience's attention with his own to the heart of the matter, and there through the medium of the work contemplates the nature of inspiration as it flows through the composition. A performance of this kind has the following distinguishing features: it has clarity, it is fundamentally calm (even when the mood requires an overlay of forceful passion); it is spacious, there is an awareness as much of the spaces between the notes as there is of the notes themselves; it is uplifting, we are taken on a journey; it gives rise to unusual thoughts of freedom and liberty, it is like being in a rarefied atmosphere high on a mountain. There is a sense of childlike simplicity and directness of perception and we may be lifted out of the usual treadmill of circling thoughts that keep us pressed down and earthbound. We may find our relentless inner commentator attempting to get back in and annotate the experience (and thus drive it away), but the strength of such a clarified performance is that we can return to those higher regions of reverie with relative ease. Here the skill of the performer in learning to use this diagram comes to the fore – the performer remains our medium through which we atune, and the audience can become ever more alert as it tunes and retunes to the fine action unfolding before it. It has frequently been noticed that through the course of a fine performance operating figure 2, there is a qualitative change in the atmosphere. One can almost feel a cool breeze wafting through. The attention becomes strengthened. An aura of warmth, almost tangibly gold, can be perceived around the performer (perhaps only a trick of the light?). Our normally turbulent breast feels calmer, more restful. A return to the street outside, or to the raucous bar is, in the first millisecond, a violent shock but we quickly accustom ourselves to a more 'normal' level of awareness.

From the performer's point of view this one little diagram does not resolve all our problems, because having learned of the possibility, tried it out and got a taste for it, it is just as quickly forgotten. Then we are back to figure 1 again, with all its useless tensions, frustrations and limitations. But once having had a taste, a knowledge of another possibility, it is possible to remember and return to the more creative situation. It is rather like two sides of a coin, you can flick it over with relative ease once you know there is something on the other side. The performer's practice is to learn to flick from side one to two *the instant you realise you have flipped back*. With practice we can begin to inhabit the world of figure 2 more and more of the time. But do not underestimate the sneakiness of figure 1. It has a great force and power for survival. Just as you are thinking how nice it is to have got to grips with 2 again, indulged in a bit of self-congratulation perhaps – Zap! You are back to circle one. But every positive effort made strengthens the ability to return and maintain for longer the link with the creative reservoir.

Now I would like to help redefine the role of the performer as artist with the aid of two more diagrams (figures 3 and 4) closely related to each other. They both call on the concept of hierarchy, a favoured view of creation in the Renaissance, though rather out of fashion today since hierarchy smacks of elitism (one of the big jargon words of our time). However, the beauty and simplicity of the concepts presented in these diagrams are such that only the most die-hard anti-elitist will

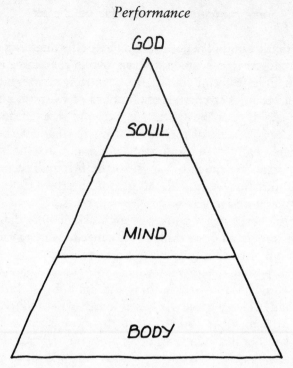

Figure 3

find it difficult. Even for them the effort will be worthwhile. The first diagram (figure 3) is basic, ancient and virtually self-explanatory. It assumes the ancient philosophic point of view that that which is more subtle interpenetrates and directs that which is more gross. It describes the movement out into ever denser creation, from God whose will to create provides the seed from which creation grows – all of creation is utterly dependent on His will. The soul is a spark of the Divine, and in that way individuated; the mind is moved by the soul to consideration of things eternal; the body is instructed on how to conduct itself directly by the mind and is dependent on it for all but the most basic movements. A problem which arises is that each lower level has an extraordinary capacity for forgetting that it is dependent on something higher. So the body gets lost in sensual appetite; the mind wanders in its own imaginings and circling fantasy; whilst the soul experiences a subtle but dull ache, knowing there is something more but not knowing how to reach for it. If this disturbing rift in the true direction of body, mind and soul is taking place much, if not most, of the time, then we are really in a sorry state. We need to re-member, that is, get our parts back in good order and functioning healthily together again. How do we make this shift? The arts have traditionally been an aid to this realignment process: philosophy is another corrector; the study of things Divine is a third. But what if the field of artistic activity is largely stemming from a misalignment, and is therefore based on false premises and only circling fantasy? Which is very frequently the case when we look about. Here, perhaps, the second diagram can help (figure 4).

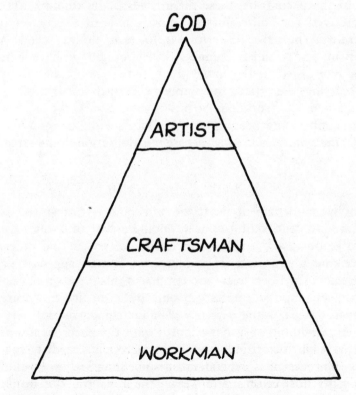

Figure 4

Essentially we have the same diagram, but the new labels afford us a different perspective. Again what is portrayed is an *ancient* view of these levels of functioning, each level being interpenetrated by the finer and more subtle levels. It places the artist in quite a different place from that in which our society tends to see him, since the nineteenth century heavily romanticised the struggling, garretcloseted artist as having some powerful inspiration of his own making. Today institutionalised art, commercial and media art, and socialist art tend to revere the artist, in a kind of undefined post-Romantic aura, with varying degrees of mainly negative results. Few of us are happy with the situation, neither the sponsor, the artist, nor the consumer.

In sharp contrast, these three levels of functioning were perceived very differently by most minds of the sixteenth century. The artist, or performer, for example was seen as a servant and considered himself as such too. But we have done the typical twentieth century thing and started at the top by discussing 'the artist', and skipped the much less interesting craftsman and workman. So now we will reverse the process, and contrast the meanings of these labels with present usage, and that which held sway before the idolisation of the artist.

WORKMAN, CRAFTSMAN AND ARTIST

Today, in Britain at least, the workman is caricatured as being indolent, skilful only in finding a way of doing least work, one hand on the shovel, pot of tea in the other, smoking a fag, and on the lookout for an approaching foreman. There are many exceptions to this gross simplification, but popular comics can only trade on this caricature because it has some currency. The craftsman, recently, has been something of a dying breed, until the phenomenon of the rebirth of craft industries – the picture is already changing. But even now the craftsman is not somebody we would look to for exciting new work of inspiration. We would expect him to be an older man, rather staid, very careful, very precise, doing a good job in a traditional way. Thank goodness this heavy picture has begun to be outdated. The artist of today has already been mentioned, but an additional point to make is that any young whizz-kid from art college, with a few of the right connections can set up his/her sculpture exhibition at this or that fashionable gallery and be described as an artist, no matter what the training, ability with techniques, etc. If it is done with enough splash, has novelty and is trendy, the work will sell, probably at quite a good price.

Now my view of these levels of functioning is not at all as jaundiced as the above caricatures suggest – I am pointing to the modern usage of these words, or labels, as they are commonly understood today. Our language is continually changing, and in many ways is becoming poorer, mainly as a reflection of the confusion of the times we live in. There is not, today, an easily stated general philosophy of the arts, which may or may not be a good thing. It does, however, contrast starkly with many other times and cultures that have had a very clear philosophy of the arts and have produced works of enduring quality which continue to inspire awe and respect. It is worth the exercise to contrast our position with others', for it might help dispel some of our confusion.

Take the view of a Leonardo, or a Michelangelo, for example, on the meaning of 'workman'. At the beginning of the sixteenth century the influence of mediaeval craft guilds was still readily apparent, and the training or schooling of many activities was conducted with a very clear sense of hierarchy. Sometimes, perhaps, there was a tendency to rigidity with too many rules, inspectors and the like. Yet the highest premium was placed on excellence. It was an honourable thing, something worthy and capable of having pride in the work to undertake the most mundane tasks, cleaning the floor, lighting the fire, preparing the raw materials, but always in the presence of the Master. Like osmosis, the young workman absorbed the influences of those more adept. Certain things became absorbed: respect for those above you;

respect for Nature (in the raw materials needed, and the processes for preparing them for use); respect for the necessary tools of whatever craft or art, so that they were always in prime condition, ready to do the best work. Not all people apprenticed were equipped to be able to advance to higher levels and to become eventually independent craftsmen. Some were destined to remain workmen alone, but with ample opportunity to take pride in the work. Others, though, advanced according to natural talent and studious application and practice. The 'journeyman' was already developing an insight into the skills of the art or craft. Eventually his 'masterpiece' was presented for inspection and judged for its craftsmanship. The independent craftsman, with a full knowledge of what it is to be a workman, could eventually take on his own apprentices. The premium placed on craftsmanship in Renaissance works is immediately obvious. Almost everything that survives, whether the most complex intarsias, or simple tools, shows a level of attainment which is quite breathtaking. However, the 'craftsman' was never confused with the 'artist' – a distinction bestowed with care. It was firmly and widely held that 'artistry' needed a lift from above, a helping hand of divine inspiration so that a life could breathe through the work that was not of any craftsman's making. The humility required for this powerful inspiration to flow tended to make the individual reticent in describing himself as an artist (others could, because they could discern the inspiration, hence the title of 'Il Divino' being bestowed on special craftsmen, now raised to the level of artist). But the attendant dangers of identifying with that label were commonly understood, the vices of sloth, arrogance, indulgence, superiority, false humility and excess were personified in numerous paintings and highlighted in tales from the oral tradition. Indeed Lucifer, the fallen angel, represented the most dramatic example of what awaits those who choose to take to themselves powers and qualities bestowed on them as gifts. These matters were the very subjects of so many paintings, poetry, and music. In settings of texts pleading for forgiveness for these very sins, the listener was reminded of the continual vigil and effort that was required. No 'artist' recognised as such by common contemporary consent could easily let this recognition go to his head – the awful warnings were everywhere.

In other ancient performing traditions, such as in the classical music of India, there was a built-in safeguard to this very problem. Each performance, at the beginning and the end, is dedicated to the artist's teacher, and his teacher before that. The invocation of long-dead masters provides a safety device against self-identification, and channels, as in figure 4, the attention of audience and performer alike to the source of inspiration itself. In John Dowland's preface, quoted on page 14, his roll-call of Linus, Orpheus, Plato (and contemporaries in other similar prefaces such as King David, Boethius and suchlike) performs a similar, almost purgative kind of function.

Fascination with 'dedication' is a recurring preoccupation for performing artists from a variety of cultures, and will reappear in various forms throughout this book. To recognise one's master, to pour libations to the appropriate gods, to make thanksgiving for past inspiration are regular reminders to the performer that he alone is insufficient for the task of entertaining.

CHAPTER THREE

The Beginning, the Middle, the End

JOHN Dee, the great Elizabethan magus, introduces the subject of numerology thus: 'O comfortable allurement, O ravishing perswasion' – an exotic language now familiar to us as being of the same quality as that of the world of performance from Renaissance times.[1] The divine play, or performance, can most easily be discerned in the power and interplay of number, which orders all creation. Dee continues:

> the Almighty and incomprehensible wisdome of the Creator, in the distinct creation of all creatures: in all their distinct partes, natures, and vertues, by order, and most absolute number, brought, from *Nothing*, to the *Formalitie* of their being and state. By *Numbers* propertie therefore, of us, by all possible meanes (to the perfection of the science) learned, we may both winde and draw ourselves into the inward and deepe search and vew, of all creatures distinct vertues, natures, properties, and *Formes*.[2]

If the art of performance is to per-form (make manifest that which exists but as yet unmanifest) then Dee's excitement about number and form has considerable relevance to us. Somehow our task is to observe the divine manifestation at play, according to the rules of number, and then perceive our own actions guided by the same laws. Renaissance thought abounded with pertinent numerological significances, perhaps the most fundamental being 'the law of three' – the beginning, the middle, and the end.[3] All actions have these three states or conditions. In this chapter we first follow the path of creation from one to three, see its laws in operation in general and particularly in performance. Then we turn to actual performance, and consider the energies which are at play, using diagram and number to pin down this elusive experience. The possibility of refinement is observed, as though a moment is frozen and inspected under a microscope, which reveals an energy-flow remarkably similar to the caduceus of Hermes. In practical application, the importance of beginning, middle, and end is considered from the point of view of the performer and audience alike. Without any direct knowledge of Renaissance numerology an audience's perception and enjoyment can be intensified or heightened by the performer's understanding.

NUMEROLOGY

Let us return to the beginning. Symbolically and graphically the point represents any and every *starting point*:

•

Here is the Divine Mind, One, at rest, all creation lying in potential, the Source of Creativity. All possibilities are held in this point, nothing in creation lies outside it. Out of this point arises division:

❘

Two represents the outward impulse to create. In an instant the object is created, and is absorbed, back into the Creator, also instantly. This position of lightning creation and absorption is unstable, yet contains all possibilities. Everything in creation is there, yet unmanifest. And so the next great numerological step is made, to three:

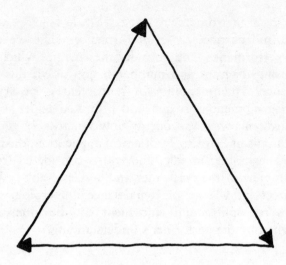

Figure 5

Here creation is expanded and maintained, the eternal, cosmic dance is in revolution, ever-moving, ever-changing, constant in continual remanifestation.

The naked simplicity of the game of numbers goes like this:

One   the divine, from which all creation arises

Two   the birth of all objects of creation, and their dissolution (regarded traditionally as the female principle of creation)

Three creation expanded and maintained in endless movement (in tradition the male principle of creation)

Four   the physical aspect of the universe, shown clearly in the four seasons, four points of the compass, the four elements, four humours

Five   the number of marriage or union (being the sum of two (female) and three (male)

Six   procreation, or generation of creation, being two times three

Seven   the fullness of a creative cycle, shown most appropriately in the seven-day week, but also in diverse more arcane matters

Eight   a return to matters and states divine, being seven plus one – the musical octave offering the most obvious example

Nine   as clothed in the nine muses – is the most perfect of numbers (three times three) and guides and inspires human endeavour.

With *Ten* we return to divinity, sometimes understood as God's representative on earth, such as the Pope, the Emperor, the King, etc. Meaning proliferates as numbers expand, and beyond the prime numbers context often creates new meanings to be read by those of understanding. It can be seen, then, that the art of numerology is a plastic art, in which you can change and adjust its meanings according to context and desire, like a sculptor working a malleable material – whatever takes your fancy, but within bounds defined by tradition, usage and observation. It is, therefore, a source of inspiration for ordering creative expression – open-ended and flexible, yet embodying ancient principles. A wonderful Renaissance example of having your cake, and eating it!

The cosmic dance of the three balanced forces has had no more beautiful symbolic manifestation than that of Sandro Botticelli's *Tre Grazie* in his inspiring *Primavera*. Three compelling ladies placed in an eternal round, for ever moving, yet serenely still with eye, head, hand, arm and body gestures so perfectly caught in still movement (balance, proportion and harmony), a model for us all to imitate. The Three Graces, borrowed from the ancient world, represent three virtues, or qualities which can be given many names. At its most fundamental perhaps we can call them Giving, Receiving and Returning (see figure 6, p. 38) which gives the foundation, through Divine Grace, of the entirety of creation.

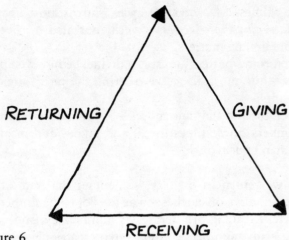

Figure 6

Related to human experience, and putting the cosmic dance right into the heart of each person's awareness, the three labels become:

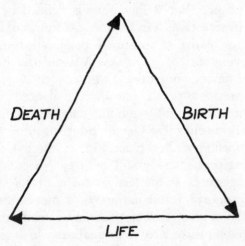

Figure 7

The life cycle, in all its complexity, may be simply observed, in endless regeneration, involving each of us, intimately, in every moment.

But when we refer the 'law of three' to artistic endeavour, and here is included the act of performance, the three forces can be called:

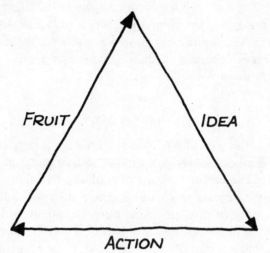

Figure 8

Now we can consider each state a little more closely. The 'idea' is a gift, an inception, not of our making. Sometimes we call it 'a bright idea'; sometimes it is feeble and dull, but that says more about our own condition than it does about the quality of the idea – we constantly search for a scapegoat for our own dullness, and blame the idea. But sometimes, in spite of ourselves perhaps, we are struck with an idea of such power and originality that we are forced out of our torpor, inspired into action. The action that follows can be of varying quality, ranging from being almost demonic and as though obsessed, to one of quiet calm, gently following each stage of the idea's manifestation. There is a vast spectrum of qualities of action in between, and all varieties can be appropriate at different stages. At some point the active stage is completed, the great work is finished, like a fruit hanging from a tree ripe for plucking. The difficulty now is letting go, for we, the artist, become so involved during many hours of skilful work that it feels as though part of ourselves is woven into the artwork. When an instrument maker has completed the final varnish, the stringing and fine tuning, and the client takes away this creation, few makers can claim to let it go easily, especially if the player might not be the best. This moment of letting go, giving up, stepping down, is in fact a moment of great release (letting the old go makes room for the new) and so the Graces continue to dance; we only have to learn to dance with them.

LETTING GO

A commonplace example, which occurred yesterday, illustrates the process, surely and with a touch of humour. The art of cooking, the *performing* art of cooking, which takes place two or three times a day can become a dreary drudgery, or can be an opportunity for divine frenzy to manifest. Reading a cookery book for instruction can be good for developing decorum, but to step off the page and allow *sprezzatura* to shape the meal can be stunning (we pass over the possibility of dreadful failures quickly). Occasionally a few crumbs of *grazia* may appear at our table. But yesterday was a clear-cut case of inspiration, the raw materials had all been bought by my wife before she went away for a weekend course on Zen meditation, I was to cook the meal for her return, and for the return of my middle daughter who was away partying in London. My youngest, Hannah, and I had a blissful meandering weekend to ourselves. Sunday afternoon was spent in preparation, clearing the kitchen, assembling the raw materials, washing, cutting and preparing the vegetables, boning the chicken and grinding the spices. The inspiration for this activity presented itself as a series of interrelated ideas, as though they were having a discussion with each other. As they conversed, I listened as I went about the more mundane tasks. The conversation ran something like this in my head.

A Zen meditation weekend is sure to mean a spartan, vegetarian weekend, which will have appealed to my wife, therefore a meal at home, though containing meat, needs to compete with the rest of the weekend's fare, and be presented delicately and very appetisingly. For Becky, party-time is not usually good food time, and she is likely to return tired (very late night) and starving, requiring an emphasis perhaps on quantity rather than quality (though she is a very discriminating eater). A third strand coursing through my mind was that of the symbol of the evening meal joining the family together in reunion (but for the eldest daughter away for a year). As many readers will know, boning a chicken is a time-consuming affair, leaving ample time for these strands of thought to interweave in a thoroughly complex web. Behind the myriad details was the idea of sustenance: of the body, in the most basic sense of refuelling; of the senses, in that sight, taste and smell should be enlivened or heightened; of the mind, enjoying the culinary creation as a concept; of the spirit, the meal symbolising sustenance of the family in love.

The afternoon flew by, as chicken was cubed, marinaded (in exotic spices, aceto balsamico, virgin oil of the finest); leek and onion sliced ready for last-minute, almost dry, fast fry; carrots cut at a unique angle to make a fresh impact in colour and shape, then soaked until time for brief boiling; potatoes diced and soaked for similar treatment but with a piece of grated cheese to add when mashing, so that it would *look* familiar on the plate but would *taste* different in the mouth; rocket washed and chopped ready for last-minute addition to the chicken, just before going on to the plate so that its intense green would be preserved; a cheese-board of the finest Stilton, whole goats cheese, Welsh ewes' milk and ripe Vacherin; tiny 'gardeners' delight' tomatoes quartered and steeped in deep-green olive oil, wine vinegar and chopped basil; a dark 62 per cent cocoasolids chocolate to round out the feast.

Time ran out during these preparations, and all was not quite ready for the actual cooking process when it was time to leave the kitchen and collect wife and daughter from the distant station. Everyone had news to tell: Hannah and I with our meanderings, Carla with stories of bells, lovely monks with shaven heads, Becky with fantastic stories of an all-niter never to be forgotten. We all wanted to hear about everything, so we agreed we would hear every detail over supper when all was settled and concentration easy.

Back home the kitchen whirled as chicken and marinade met hot oil. The steam, the spitting oil and the roar of unlike substances meeting was like an alchemist's furnace; the potatoes bubbled alongside the carrots, the leek and onion slices met the almost dry pan. Everything was stirred, shaken, mixed, drained, with the dexterity of a dancer from the New York Contemporary Ballet. In the midst of this, I, the performer, was thoroughly enjoying this moment of un-doubted *sprezzatura* as all was about to be served. The rocket had just been stirred into the chicken when the telephone rang – Abigail, the eldest, phoning from Florence with important travel news, flight times, ticket numbers, etc. There is no frustration like that of the interrupted artist-cook, hanging on to the concept of this carefully timed creation (seeing in the mind's eye the rocket wilting and loosing its vivid green). By trying to hurry the telephone call in inform-ing Abigail that food was about to be served, the obvious rejoinder was flung petulantly across the airwaves: 'You only think about your stomach, and care not at all for your daughter', who of course felt homesick, and wanted, at that moment, to be home joining in this feast.

With a little more patience and judicious handling, the call was decently over, the meal was brilliantly served, and all sat down at table. Now the cook expected delirious noises of 'Ooh' and 'Aah' as this symbolic creation reached its (tem-porary) destination. The artist was to be frustrated, for the conversation waxed intensely about meditation weekends, a different lifestyle, people looking freshfaced and eager, hours of meditation, and (final blow to artist's pride) meals were eaten in complete silence, and the food tasted *so good*! As the telling became ever more animated the meal on the plate became colder, less appetising and little tasted.

The reader must, at this point, allow for artistic exaggeration, because in fact an independent observer would confirm that the meal was enjoyed by all, but the perceptions of the chef were clouded by the identification with the hours of effort gone into this creation. He was not able to give up the fruit of his labours and this was pointed up with nice irony by the very tale of eating in silence. The event didn't meet the details of the personalised picture of the meal held in the cook's mind yet it did satisfy the fundamental concept which fired the whole activity – the family was sustained on all levels. Here was an essential balance, but the artist had to learn to give up 'his' creation more readily. The eternal dance continues, we simply have to learn the right steps at the right moment.

AUDIENCE AND PERFORMER

We will now look more closely at energies at play in the more formal performance situation, when the audience play an equal role to the performer. The attention of both parties is the chief means by which energy is focussed, and naturally the point of focus for both is on the work which is unfolding (that is, taking a span of time to manifest). The time taken is an important part of the equation, for in that time from the beginning, through the middle, to the end, a metamorphosis may take place. Some kind of transformation is experienced. Figure 9 (p.44) helps identify what is going on, creating the idea of performing energies as a mirror-image: The upper triangle represents the performer, the lower, the audience. Number 1 is the giving of attention to 2 which is the work in progress, which takes a time. Number 3 is an internalising of that shared experience, a taking inside, even a 'taking to heart'. Both performer and audience meet in 2, internalise independently, and then return the attention again, refined by the process. As the work is still going on, the movement round happens uncountable times, for this energy flow is very fast. It must have a speed, I suppose, but I doubt

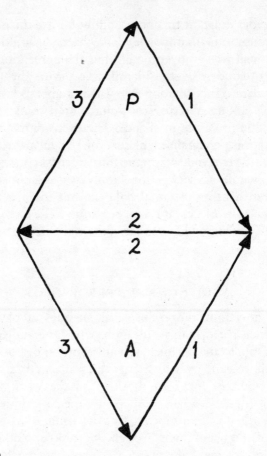

Figure 9

it could ever be measured since the subjective experience is infinitely variable. It is probably much faster than sound, and may be faster than light, but such comparisons are useless for it is like comparing chalk and cheese.

The beginning of the work, let's say a piece of music, begins in silence – the quality and length of which will vary depending on the nature of the piece to follow, the artist, the audience, the space with its size, shape and acoustical properties, and the time of day. Then the work unfolds, out of that silence, with attention joining the efforts of the performer with that of the audience. Finally, the work ends in silence, the quality and length of which will vary, with the same list of variables as at the beginning, but with an important addition, the quality and nature of the music which has gone before which changes the perception of silence. In this moment the transformation becomes almost tangible, and may be highly charged. How we move out of that 'distilled' silence will depend on habit, custom, embarrassment, relief, and all the other previously listed variables. This distilled moment we will return to in our study.

The next diagram takes a slightly different point of view on the same situation which emphasises the energy *cycle* of the performing situation:

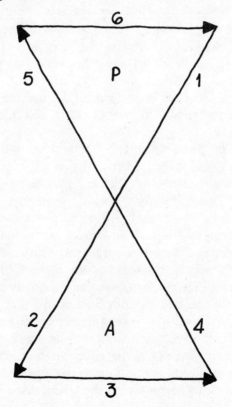

Figure 10

The performer and audience still occupy respectively the upper and lower triangles, but now the attention is symbolized by the point where the two triangles meet, at their apex. The performer *gives* his attention to set the work in motion, at 1. The audience *receives* that impetus at 2, internalises it and *transforms* it at 3. Now transformed or heightened, the audience *returns* this energy at 4, which is *received*, at 5, by the performer who in turn internalises and *transforms* that attention at 6.

This diagram is like a frozen moment in performance, like an arrested action in a film, which allows us to stop and inspect in detail something which is so fleeting. There are so many frames per second in film, yet nothing compared to the number of 'frames' in a live performance. As soon as the realisation of the movement from 1 to 6 has dawned, the next cycle from 7 to 12 has completed – it is an instantaneous experience. The high artificiality of making this momentary cross-section is typical of the work the student has to do under *decoro*. Once the concept is established, however, the performer and audience can begin to relax and enjoy the play which unfolds.

A student on a course in The Hague when introduced to this diagram asked if the cycle could also work in a negative way, that is, could one see the energy running down, or seizing up. Then followed a good few minutes of strong, negative energy discussion. It always surprises me (and used to disturb, but now amuses), how eager we are to latch on to downward cycles. There is a thrill in the chase of negative energy spirals which lights us up for a short time with a demonic kind of enthusiasm, but then burns us up, leaving the opposite of 'an ecstatic transport of divine frenzy'. Yes, there can be downward spirals in the performing experience, but they do not need practising, they are well capable of looking after themselves. What does need practice is the ever-sharpened alertness for joining an upward spiralling energy, to work in harness with the 'caduceus' of Mercury.

His central rod with opposed intertwining serpents has the power to destroy and enhance creativity. The choice is actually ours.

Every transformation journey, outlined in this instance through the example of a performance, and discussed via means of diagrams, has a destination, or resolution. In this case the two triangles balanced on their apex begin to merge, as the gaze of the inner eye of performer and audience becomes steadier. I relate a frequently recurring personal experience to illustrate the interaction. As a lute player, working with an instrument whose every note decays rapidly into silence after a sharp initial attack, the task is as much to control the spaces between the notes as the quality of the notes themselves. (Actually I sense this may be true of all music-making, but the nature of the lute enforces this aware-ness.) During the course of the unfolding of a rambling Renaissance lute fantasia it is quite remarkable how the silences beging to deepen (if time, place, acoustics and I allow it) as the work proceeds. Such is the intensification of attention that it seems my fingers pluck the strings under the direction of the audience. In other words, that *I* am simply observing, the audience *becomes* the performer, the perfor-mer *becomes* the auditor. In these moments time stands still; each note has an eternal quality; there is no possibility of error. Figure 11, shows what takes place; the two triangles merge, by the apex moving up for the audience, down for the performer. This ancient symbol, identified, long after its widespread use, with the Jewish faith, is the symbol of balance, harmony, the uniting of opposites – heaven on earth. This particular manifestation of 'as above, so below' shows without compromise the potential of performance – a state of bliss which can be shared by all those with ears to hear. The speedy movement of the energy cycle diagram gives place to a steady, held contemplation leaving performer and audience alike in a rapt ecstasy.

This then, is the potential, and it does happen – I have witnessed it. So too have you, the reader, if you have

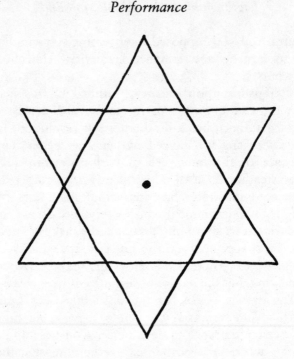

Figure 11

stayed with the book this far. Now we can acknowledge the potential of performance, without embarrassment. We can continue our efforts to dive deeper in so that we can become more useful conductors of this wonderful energy transformation. At the beginning, the middle and the end we have different roles to play, both as audiences and as performers. Let us consider this further, for this book is to educate the audience quite as much as educate the performer.

There are many ways of beginning, indeed every beginning of its nature is new, first-born. Every beginning arises from One:

●

As audience and performer become more attuned to this simple truth, the more the performing space is filled with awe and wonder. In the beginning ... (there are then uncountable ways of completing the sentence) ... there is utter rest, utter silence ... from which the performance begins to manifest. In the symbolic beginning of creation as represented by the beginning of the performance we need some simple techniques to exercise ourselves with. And the simpler they are, the more effective they will be. Like taking a breath, simply but consciously without interference, following the movement of air into the nostrils, filling the lungs, the expanding of the breast, the enjoyment of the apex of the breath (its sweetness, its fullness), and then the relaxation as the breath is clearly expelled, like a stream, through the lips. (We will perceive that this action too has its beginning, middle, and end.)

This simple technique for beginning a performance clearly is not always easy to do when several hundred people are watching your every quiver. The opportunities for interference are legion, and in the course of time we try them all, getting in our own way. There is nothing worse for an audience getting off to a bad start than watching a performer *trying* to take a relaxed breath. Sitting bolt upright, stiff and awkward, telling himself to RELAX. The audience takes the lead from the performer, it is the way it is. On the other hand, with an experienced artist an initial breath can be worn with such natural ease that the entire audience takes up the gentle invitation to be still, almost without noticing. Such ease comes only from long observation, careful study and constant practice.

There are many techniques to be explored by the performer to help make a clean beginning. Let the attention run to the sounds in the room, use the ears to tune up. This can be disguised by attentive tuning of the instrument, listening to each note or chord for its quality, and following its sound to the far corners of the room, encompassing all the other sounds which are contained in that space on the way (someone turning the programme; another clearing the throat; the end of a pre-concert conversation; a latecomer finding a seat; the clicking of a cooling, or heating up, light unit; the ventilation system). Let the sounds of the instrument being tested 'embrace' all other sounds, not exclude them. The audience truly delight in an artful tuning up, yet will suffer an ugly tuning period.

Another procedure is to use the eyes. Extend your sight-lines to the far corner of the room, right to the dimly-lit recesses and encircle the audience with your vision. Moving further in, towards oneself, the eyes might meet those of another individual, perhaps someone who is ready to smile in recognition of this moment's importance, or someone who needs a little reassurance that it is all right to relax. Then the eyes of the front row, who are there because they chose to be there – sitting on the front row is a *very* conscious choice. These people deserve careful attention and a smile perhaps (certainly better, in most instances, than a stern encounter). Time enough if the work you are to play is profoundly elegiac to turn the mood from smiles to mourning – this is only the beginning!

Other possibilities abound. Every time you enter the per-forming space new discoveries are made, for you have, truly, never been in that time/space before. Underlying these specific examples, breath, sound and sight, is the desire to commune. The senses were regarded, in the sixteenth century and earlier, as the windows to the soul. Use your windows then for your soul to commune with the souls of the audience. You, the performer, set the pace, but the audience is (mostly) willing to follow. Having worked through an appropriate beginning, it is time for that to come to an end. There is, now, a silence, a stillness which may last a milli-second, or an age – nothing moves, for this is a moment of clarity and focus – and then the work begins in a kind of spontaneous combustion. All the preparation is over; now full focus on the work to be done. The sage's image of the still millpond into which is dropped a good-size pebble describes well the effect of the opening note or gesture. There is a moment to start which is in harmony with the performer, the audience, the space, the time. With experience that knowledge or sense of when to place the first sound or movement becomes ever more sure.

Then we are off! Action piles on action, and the performer is in a state of maximum concentration which directs the attention of the entire audience. There surely is an analogy with the start of a race. All contestants, in peak training, 'At the ready! Get set! Go!' The starter pistol explodes, snapping the tension and the race begins. As it happens, in music and dance, the starter pistol is silent, but there is no doubt in anyone's mind who is present when the performer has chosen *exactly* the right moment to begin. Yet another analogy comes to mind for the time span of 'the middle' – that of the arrow from the bow. The archer releases, at the optimum moment, and the arrow then flies with a volition, once released, out of anyone's guidance. A breeze may deflect it, its flight feathers may be askew, but no one can affect its flight, once released. The analogy holds good for the performance which is under way, for there is a sense that the work unfolds in the moment of presentation without interference. But the arrow is a simple device without a human mind, whereas the performer and work are complex entities with ample room for interference and guidance. Nevertheless, the human agency would do well to recall the flight of the arrow in its simplicity as a model of a clean activity.

The 'middle' work is complex and varied – in fact, infinitely varied, for no two performances are alike. The awareness of the performer operates on several levels at once, linked together it would seem by the discipline of performing alone. The *body* level frequently takes care of itself, though posture and muscle tensions can be eased or worsened by the mind entering body level. The *senses* may be more or less awake. In their gross aspect, one or other sense dominates over the others. In music it would be natural for the aural sense to be more forward than the sense of smell, for example, but in the subtle region of the senses there is often a different hierarchy. A subtle sense of taste may be directing many of the momentary decisions as the music unfolds, especially if there is an element of improvisation in the performance. *Sprezzatura* itself is guided by good taste.

When it comes to the region of *mind*, then variation and division abound. The mind is a complex fugue where fantasy and imagination play counterpoint to fears and desires. If the musician believes he spends years training his body to respond to the tiniest motor actions, then he needs lifetimes to bring the mind to the simplest discipline, and do it reliably. Nevertheless, it is part of our God-given equipment, and we must attempt the impossible. In actual performance the mind does the most bizarre things, like remembering what you had for breakfast, or thinking what you might eat after the concert, or wondering if you did remember to do up your flies before walking on, or 'I wonder what that important potential sponsor three rows from the back is thinking of this stunning piece?', 'Why has that idiot critic come yet again to write his arrant nonsense?', 'Will the plane be late tomorrow?', 'Did Dowland really intend that dissonance?', 'And did he ever actually meet Marenzio in Rome?'.

The mindless chatter of encircling thoughts is present even when the music is at its most sublime, and at its most technically challenging. Nevertheless, the nature of the unfolding performance is that it is happening in real time, now and presents us with a powerful opportunity to 'cut the crap' – that is, circling thoughts may be there in abundance, but there is the energy to let them drop. In this the act of performing is a meditation, and should the performer choose he may pierce to the stiller levels of mind and observe from the level of *soul*. Here the bubbling activity of mind can be observed, from here the conscious decision can be made: let the mind play like an infant when it matters not, but act like an adult in moments of consequence, with a full responsibility. The music in this or that moment demands your better judgment, the higher self is engaged, and the playful rubbish is instantly discarded. Perhaps the music requires this, or that, characterisation – from a high vantage point of observation the appropriate mask can be chosen, donned, and the 'persona' fills the stage. These moments of real play move us to our very foundations.

And so to 'the end'. All this effort comes to a close, and in the last note or movement there is a point where action and sound cease. This, though, for the performer is not yet the end of the end, for on into the silence there is still a duty. The performer's antennae are at full alert, still but vibrant, the entire room is as though at full stretch. It is the performer's task to sense when that alert rest should be disturbed. A moment too soon, we all feel cheated; a moment too late, it becomes affected or an embarrassment. There is often in the audience a demon clapper who likes to show he recognises a final cadence, and the final fruit of the work can be mulched by his misplaced enthusiasm. We have to let that pass too, though live in hope that we are training a more alert audience for the future. Should a demon clapper be reading these words, please take careful note.

CHAPTER FOUR

Characterisation

AN ardent Japanese student soprano asked me recently, after a lecture on performance, if I had meant that one must become 'as though not there, blank?' The answer is both 'yes' and 'no', and with her desire to please and be a good student, it was very important she understood the paradox properly, for a sterile emptiness could lead to the dullest of dutiful performances. I asked her to prepare a particular song, 'Fine knacks for ladies' by John Dowland, which is a paradoxical choice for a young Japanese girl to sing – the words are of an Elizabethan pedlar or quack-doctor, offering his wares at the Fair, 'but for the fair to view', and he is a slick salesman, a rascal, with a sense of humour and a good turn of phrase. In fact the song and the singer were worlds apart, culturally, emotionally and in personality.

However, the struggle for this girl in creating a performance which entertained and convinced the hundred or so people in the workshop audience is what lies at the heart of this chapter on characterisation – as performers we have to learn to play a part as fully and as appropriately as possible. For the world of theatre and actors much of what I have to say here is self-evident, but for the world of music, including instrumentalists and singers, so much attention goes to instrument and technique that the first elements of stagecraft are unknown. Even for the actor, though, there is a philosophy of performing which may be refined, especially by calling on ancient modes of thought to develop our perceptions.

As players in life's drama, we wear a mask, often unconsciously. That is, we believe our part to be real. The performer who is growing needs to understand his mask, the one adorning him from birth, so that other parts can be played when appropriate. The person needs to distance himself from 'personality', so that the 'persona' can be more readily adopted as required. To be exhorted that we become like an empty vessel in order to resound God's praises more fully is fine, yet even the vessel is made of particular materials, metal, clay, wood or leather and is made of a certain shape, size and thickness. All this individualises the resounding the vessel makes in praise of the Divine. Personality is one aspect of the dimensions of the performer's vessel, to be used when appropriate, to be studied and worked as much as the aspects of the body. One difficulty set in our way is that personality and ego fuse together easily and distort or dominate our presentation. The small self colours, inhibits or belittles the large self and this leaves us less free to adopt the appropriate 'persona' for a particular performance. The more conscious we become of our entire nature and learn to observe ourselves at work, the more consciously we can choose appropriate action. Though we can never see ourselves as others see us, we can become less blind to our weaknesses and defects, more alert to our strengths and qualities and eventually learn to direct what we are to better account in performance.

The metaphorical mask of which I speak has of course its counterpart in physical masks donned from ancient times for sacred and theatrical ritual. In integrated cultures, such as the aborigine or Amazon indian, there is no differentiation between sacred and theatrical. Ancient high civilisations too kept a close link between the two, especially in the use of and belief in the mystical power of the mask. After a few hundred years of compartmentalising we are perhaps beginning to return to a more integrated view of ourselves and the rest of creation, of the sacred and secular aspects of our being. The mask may be a profoundly important means back to this synthesis.

It is unnecessary for me to attempt here a brief history of the use and abuse of the mask, from prehistory, its use in shamanism, through Greek theatre, in tragedy and in comedy, its rise in sixteenth century commedia dell'arte in Italy, its effete use in French eighteenth century pantomime, to the revival in a disturbingly modern way with the masks of Werner Strub of Basle. There are a number of good surveys written by experts in this field to which the interested reader should turn.[1] My interest lies with the physical mask only in so much as it advances our awareness of the metaphorical mask. I consider the mask an essential symbol for the successful performer.

For the expert player in the mask tradition the relationship of player to mask becomes an intensely mystical experience. Codes of behaviour assume religious intensity, and superstitions abound. Much of the lore relating to maskwearing is of truly ancient lineage in a tradition which links our time with pre-Christian pagan cults and mysteries. I have had the good fortune to work closely on several occasions with the Italian 'commedia dell'arte' troupe 'La Famiglia Carrara' directed by its present leader, Titino Carrara.[2] There have been many hours of delightful rehearsal and performance spent with this team – some of the most inspiring and creative in my career as a performer. Their theatrical tradition goes back ten generations, 350 years, as one family, but of course they are one branch of the mainstream 'commedia' art which links back to pre-Roman times. The force of this pedigree can be felt in their every gesture and in their unerring use of mask. I will focus on one mask in particular which especially fascinates me – the *zanni* mask. The one I have was given me by Titino, who plays various *zanni*'s, including the most famous manifestation, *Arlecchino*. With the gift he said I didn't really need the mask, because I had been a *zanni* in a previous incarnation, but it was just to remind me. I took this as a compliment, from a venerable tradition, despite the fact that we get our word 'zany' or 'crazy' from this character!

Recent tradition (about 500 years) has the 'zanni' speaking

in a very strong, vulgar *bergamasca* dialect. The family of zannis are serving men of the lowest social order, servants tantamount to slaves.[3] They serve the higher social orders, namely Pantalone, the aged, decrepit, repulsive Venetian patriarch; or the Dottore, the learned fool from Padova or Bologna, who has read so many books on every subject, but gets them all confused together and speaks in a macaronic style incorporating Paduan dialect, Latin and occasionally Greek. Both these buffoons wear very individual, traditional masks, quite bizarre to behold. But I stay with a closer study of the servant, Zanni. His clothes are of the simplest, roughest cloth, often torn and dishevelled. His masters are too mean with money to buy him anything finer. Not that Zanni is troubled by his appearance, for his concerns are more basic – essentially food and sex – but he approaches life with a good will and a sense of humour. He carries, stuffed in his belt, a 'spade', a wooden object with a handle and two flexible 'blades' which slap together and make a very loud noise when he biffs Pantalone, or anyone else around, on the behind. This prop has become known as a 'slapstick', and has of course given its name, unconsciously, to an entire area of 'custard-pie' comedy. Zanni makes his 'spade' stand in for a spade, a sword, a spear, a penis, a 'bambino' and anything else that may be required. It is his only prop, his only possession.

Zanni's mask is made of leather, is dark brown and stops below the nose, leaving the actor's mouth free to be vigorously expressive. The nose is broad and pushed upward, like the lower primates. The eyes are small black circular holes, not only for the actor to see, but also for the spirit of the mask to pour out. Above the eyes are two little tufts of hair for eyebrows. On the forehead, to the left side, is a small bump with a bright blood-red circle in the centre. This, tradition has it, was the devil's horn, which was cut off when he became enslaved. The whole appearance is very benign but bestial, particularly monkey-like. The character of Zanni is summed up in his mask – he represents the beast in man, he reminds us of our primeval origins, he has no time for fancy breeding, airs or graces. Zanni has no malice in him, yet he is spurned by everyone (except Franceschina, the low-born serving maid played by a man in drag). Zanni is the 'action' man in most commedia plots – around him the drama turns – he represents the very lifeforce of creation, in its most pagan manifestation.

The entire force of 'commedia dell'arte', when played with the abandon of the 'Famiglia Carrara' brings the ancient world into our consciousness. Here is tradition, in service to improvised drama, presenting us with barely clothed human archetypes. We are at the fount of Pan and our blood courses with a primeval energy.

Zanni would seem a far cry from Dowland's pedlar, a creation of an effete court, yet they have more than might appear in common. The reserved Japanese girl might feel embarrassed to consider the earthy, vulgar energy of Zanni in helping her shape her lute song, yet in her own culture, in Kabuki, there is a very strong tradition with extraordinarily close parallels to 'commedia dell'arte'. Grotesque forest creatures, barely human, reflect the animistic spirituality which is embedded in the Japanese psyche, and these are fellow creatures to Zanni. For the performer who has attempted to face some of the long forgotten denizens of the forest in himself, there spreads out an immensely valuable store of archetypes to inform his performance.

PLAYING THE PART

Let us turn again, in contrast to vulgar Zanni, to the world of the Elizabethan lute song, with its wonderful heritage of fine lyric poetry inspired, via Ariosto and Sannazaro, by the Roman lyricists, Ovid, Virgil, Horace and others. What now follows is a series of observations on the use of this repertoire specifically in relation to characterisation.

First, a reminder of how *fully* you have to play a part, and this applies to all performances, in any medium, or any era, vocal, instrumental, dance, theatre.

This essential requirement can be seen with particular clarity in the English song repertoire in the first half of the seventeenth century. The reason being that lyric poetry, though mainly anonymous, is so finely expressed and so clearly characterised. It is also a body of material easily referred to, gathered in one standard modern edition (E. H. Fellowes *English Madrigal Verse*).[4] The music is not quite so easy to refer to, with numerous old editions from the beginning of this century being reprinted in seemingly modern packaging, but transposed into peculiar keys, and even more peculiar piano parts. The standard edition is again, E. H. Fellowes *The English Lute Song Series* (Stainer and Bell)[5] but best of all is to refer to the facsimile reprints of the original publications (Brian Jordan).[6] With these the modern student is faced with precisely the same image as the original performers – this must be a good starting point.

It is not enough for the performer to 'be yourself' in performance, namely, well-prepared, disciplined, technically fluent and assured (*decoro*); nor to rely on being lively, engaging, able to take risks (*sprezzatura*). You have to be yourself playing a part appropriate to the work in hand. I have seen lute songs performed to a very high standard by a personality so colourful, such a character in himself, that whatever song he sang the listener was aware of him first, always the same likeable chap – the character of the song was obliterated.

The performer is first the *servant* of the work (which part is learned through study). Secondly, he is the work's *mouthpiece* in the moment of performance (that is, the representative, or advocate for the work). Third, the performer is the *collector of the trophies*. This may seem an odd way of saying 'taking the applause', but its oddity helps us to understand that the applause, delight or gratitude expressed at the end of a performance is only in part addressed to the performer. Much of it is addressed to the work itself, but the performer has to collect the garlands.

The position of the performer is essentially dutiful, full of love and admiration for the work (if there is not such respect then perhaps that performer should not be performing that work). Though there needs to be love and admiration, the performer must stay impartial, for only then can the characterisation be strong.

The entire English lute song repertoire can be seen as falling into twelve different characterisations:

(1)   innocent joy
(2)   amorous joy
(3)   intent to seduce
(4)   successful lover
(5)   jealous lover
(6)   angry lover
(7)   lover's melancholy
(8)   self-lover's melancholy
(9)   despair melancholy
(10) denial of the world melancholy
(11) Platonic love
(12) devotional love

Now these categories are not intended to be the *only* way to see this repertoire – another mind might see thirteen, fourteen, fifteen or a hundred categories. But the principle is clear, you must define the general nature of an individual song and have a feeling for how it fits into the overall repertoire. The unique quality of a song cannot be appreciated without understanding it in relation to its fellows.

When going through the exercise of categorising, one's perception shifts and changes. For the purposes of this instance I chose twelve categories because it is a good Renaissance number – they perceived humanity in twelve basic psychological types (being 3 [man] times 4 [the humours and elements]). Reflected of course, in the zodiac and planetary influences. ('As above, so below'). Man was regarded as being *The Twelve Wonders of the World* according to one of the lute song books of that title, made of twelve light-hearted verses on the petty foibles of men and women.[7]

The effort of categorising is a good discipline for it encourages one to begin to think in a mode of thought-patterning which gets a little closer to the way the poet and composer perceived their relationship to creation. The Elizabethan backcloth of thought was so very different from our own. 'Peculiar' is the word used by E. M. W. Tilyard in his book *The Elizabethan World Picture*, where he forges a remarkable structuring of thought which gave rise to the genius of that age.[8] The performer owes it to that peculiar and powerful time to approach their mind-set with care and respect.

Let us expand a little on the twelve categories of the lute song: as presented they form a logical satisfying cycle, from (1) to (12) – a cycle which might raise a smile, for it is decidedly a downward trend, until at least numbers (11) and (12). It is a sequence we might recognise immediately from our own experience. The list implies that all songtexts are about matters of love (most are, but not quite all). So this inadequacy in the list of twelve suggests, perhaps, another perspective on the repertoire:

(a) amorous (including erotic and devotional)
(b) political/historical (works created to meet a specific need in time and place)
(c) pastoral (frequently amorous, but not exclusively so)

These three conventions interplay with the twelve categories, giving a very large number of possible secondary or tertiary layers of categorising. All possible permutations need to interplay, so there is no need to be hasty in pinning down a song to this or that mood or category. This exercise can be very subtle and may take some time. It is not, in any way, a closed system I have suggested, but a guide.

There is another factor in the equation of categorisation in relation to the performance – oneself. We, according to Renaissance psychology, have twelve basic moods which shift and change according to time, place, season and lunar cycle. We certainly are not constant. Therefore, the dictum *nosce teipsum* (know thyself) should be at the centre of the performing artist's creed, reiterated daily. The art of performing can be an aid to following this dictum. The detailed categorisation of ourselves is not something to enter in depth here – should we use a modern psychological vocabulary to discuss this, and if so, which school: Behavioural, Jungian or Hillmanic? Or should we continue with a sixteenth century focus and consider balance and imbalance between yellow and black bile, or the virtues of sanguine against choleric dispositions? In any case, the point is that *self-observation* is essential to the performer, in order that a finer knowledge of one's own changing condition can temper the specific performance of the work in hand.

Here is a reminder of the amazing variety of factors in the development of the characterisation of a particular lute song:

(i)   a twelve-part ordering of the repertoire
(ii)   overlaid, from a different perspective, with a three-part view of basic conventions
(iii)   humanity, in general, is in twelve basic personality types
(iv)   the performer, being one of these, comes in twelve varying moods, or colours

So how do we make use of this mass of shifting material? By asking ourselves some fundamental questions about what we need to equip ourselves with in the moment of performance – this must be our examination point.

We certainly need *decoro*, *sprezzatura*, and an awareness of *grazia*. But in addition we need to develop:

(*a*)   *A sense of style* – meaning, of course, historical style and an ever-finer awareness of how 'they' would have performed (which brings in all aspects of the 'authentic' movement), but also going way beyond that into every aspect of 'style' in a conceptual sense. The assured performer develops a sense of style which is instantly recognisable, but never gets in the way for its own sake.

(*b*) A *sureness of delivery* – to do with confidence, certainly, but also to do with authority, and relaxedness (the image of the arrow from the bow comes to mind again).

(*c*) *Clarity of gesture in eye, head, hand, arm, body* – this is not exclusive to Renaissance or Baroque gestures, though it incorporates that repertoire. This essential clarity is more fundamental, the performer becoming aware of the power of body language as a means of communication, and characterisation.

(*d*) A *sense of timing* – knowing exactly when to respond with appropriate action or when to desist from action – when to start, when to stop, and every action between.

(*e*) *Variety of intensity* – intensity of all kinds; not just volume and speed but emotional intensity, sense of line and the breaking of the line, not missing the powerful moments on the journey, giving every note a purposefulness and direction, yet being gentle at times and not always pressing.

(*f*) A *response to changing moods of the moment* – letting the unexpected influence your performance, so that your prepared approach is not necessarily the only solution – the moment informs the characterisation.

(*g*) To *laugh, and to sigh (and all other appropriate responses) convincingly, as though you were feeling these things yourself* – lesson one for the actor, but a novel idea for the musician. An ability to take the dominant moods and affects of the work and respond as if they were your own feelings.

After all this endeavour, when you can play the role you have elaborated through a combination of study and experience, there is a tendency to begin to believe in it, so that you think you are it. You forget that you are playing a role, and habit takes over. Repetition obviously breeds that kind of relationship, but as soon as habit takes over, the characterisation begins to die. We need to be ever more aware, when performing, of when to be still, when to be silent, when to stop acting. Then our characterisation arises afresh, new every time.

CHAPTER FIVE

The Orpheus within

IT is necessary to know melancholy, in its many moods, claims Marsilio Ficino, in order to touch the hearts of the audience and fire their spirits with an Orphic frenzy. Ficino should know. By all accounts, and particularly that of his chief patron, Lorenzo de' Medici (who saw Orpheus reborn in Marsilio), the Medici philospher was granted, in common consent by his contemporaries, a rare power of divine furore. Ficino had touched the Orpheus within himself, and revealed it to those who came in contact with him. No doubt Ficino had his detractors, especially from within the orthodox church, but few men of any period can have been more whole-heartedly loved than he. Yet many of his ardently held tenets strike us as very strange today.

This question of melancholy being a required state of mind in order to advance to a more subtle awareness is a case in point. But Marsilio, with his Age, was sure of this point. Indeed for two or three generations after Marsilio, the concept of inspired melancholy was elaborated, to find its fullest flowering in England around 1600, and particularly in John Dowland, who, as we already know, was called the 'English Orpheus'.

I now suspect that only a full understanding of the various manifestations of melancholy, as understood by Renaissance culture, will reveal the hermetically hidden meanings in much Renaissance art, and particularly in the neo-Platonic flowering so carefully cultivated by Ficino and his followers. The secret to their understanding of Orpheus and all his related mythology, including a philosophy of the performing arts, lies in probing melancholy and the unlikely concept of 'black bile', one of the four juices of the body (the others being blood, phlegm, and yellow bile) that gave rise to the 'humours'. This dismal sounding subject is far from being all gloom. In fact being a basically optimistic, cheerful chap myself, I find much to excite, and even amuse. This study is full of paradox, perhaps even depends on it − certainly nothing is quite what it seems.

This probing into black bile begins with a quotation from Thomas Kyd's *The Spanish Tragedy*. Hieronimo sets a dismal scene:

> There is a path upon your left-hand side,
> That leadeth from a guilty conscience
> A darksome place and dangerous to pass:
> There shall you meet with melancholy thoughts,
> Whose baleful humours if you out uphold,
> It will conduct you to despair and death:
> Whose rocky cliffs when you have once beheld,
> Within a hugy dale of lasting night,
> That, kindled with the world's iniquities,
> Doth cast up filthy and detested fumes.
>   (III, xi, 13−23)[1]

What a 'melancholy region of despair' is this? Such powerful language the Elizabethan playwrights had, and with every black sentence one feels that they have been there and done that. They know what they write from personal experience. The solitariness of this scene conjures Hell and Damnation, as though Orpheus was just entering Hades. Or is it the barren desert where, empty-handed, having given in to his desire to see Euridice, he banished himself for endless years only to sing a melancholy wail, heard by none but the little nightingale, and finally the murderous Bacchantes?

Kyd's lines have a relevance to Orpheus, within the general melancholy tradition, but let us first move closer to the tradition itself, before focussing on Orpheus specifically. Kyd's unique lines belong entirely within established tradition, he invigorates commonplace dramatic images. Likewise the lines that Dowland sets, in mellifluously jarring notes, are a unique example of a familiar groan:

> In darkness let me dwell, the ground shall sorrow be;
> The roof despair to bar all cheerful light from me;
> The walls of marble black that moistened still shall weep;
> My music hellish jarring sounds to banish friendly sleep.
> Thus wedded to my woes, and bedded to my tomb,
> O let me living, living die, till death do come.[2]

Such words, set to such notes from our English Orpheus places melancholy deep into our hearts. But melancholy on this inspired level enters deep in, and affects our condition profoundly, indeed changes us permanently. The philosophy for this is another commonplace: the Lady Music, seated on a cloud half-way between Heaven and Earth with a lute in her hands and an open songbook on her knee (see the title-page of Dowland's *First Booke of Songs*, 1597, for a well-established emblem) is never happier than when her musicians on earth are performing melancholy music. The Lady Mirth, with her cheerful song delights for a moment and then her influence evaporates. Melancholy music, performed with inspiration, changes the listener's condition fundamentally.

Melancholy was not always treated with such respect, in fact the subject was a goldmine of humorous caricatures – such as Jacques in *As you like it*, or as desperately driven satanic characters like Hamlet. The literature of the time is filled with incredible, wild creations inspired by melancholy. The humoral doctrine which gave rise to it was essentially simple, and good sound subjective medicine (even if objectively disproved today). The conditions of humanity were a mixture of hot, cold, moist and dry, in changing proportions. This gave rise to the four types of humour: sanguine, choleric, phlegmatic and melancholic, that were permanently in flux. All of them had their character portrayals in theatre,

but none more so than melancholy, partly because such a
persona had become fashionable in the England of the 1590s,
so there was much mileage to be had from topical comment.
Jacques gives seven types of melancholic: the scholar, the
lover, the musician, the lawyer, the courtier, the lady, and
finally himself, the traveller. All of them could be ridiculed
without difficulty. More traditionally there were four types:
the scholar; the musician; the lover; the madman – each
having their appropriate emblems: a large book; a lute; hand
on the heart; dishevelled hair, hat and clothes. Of course
more than one kind of melancholic could be found in the
same person.

In addition certain stock, and somewhat predictable, images were linked with the various melancholy types: night,
darkness, graveyards, owls, bats, cats, dogs, hares and deer
(because they are solitary), the yew and cypress, lead, black
floppy hat, folded arms, pale skin and so on.[3]

Certain standard conditions would be associated with
melancholy: a tendency to introspection, antisocial postures,
delusion, visionary speech, a general discontent, self-
indulgence, superiority, calculating, etc. Often in a theatrical
context, the melancholic believed in himself whilst everyone
else, cast and audience alike, found him a source of amuse-
ment. Only the female melancholic could be taken seriously,
for some reason.

Perhaps with this cult of overblown melancholy we can
observe a society protecting itself from a rather difficult
tendency, namely, that much profound art, which often
sailed close to the orthodox wind, was initiated by those of a
natural melancholic inclination. It was a safety-valve which
allowed fun to be made, whilst still being a body of truly
worthwhile material for serious contemplation.

Some of the finest poets of the age contributed consider-
ably to the genre of literary melancholy, and in England the
vivacious Lucy, Countess of Bedford, provided a focal point
for dark studies.[4] Her patron saint, St. Lucy, was a second
century Christian martyr whose particularly gruesome form

of torture was to have had both eyes gouged out, only to be miraculously restored the next day. To commemorate her sightless agony, throughout the Middle Ages and Renaissance, she was depicted carrying a plate with two eyeballs resting on it. Ironically, her name of course means light – a paradox not wasted on such as George Chapman and John Donne who were of the Lucy Bedford circle. They and their contemporaries delighted in creating a 'school of darkness' around the lucent Countess of Bedford. Enigmatic poems revolving around eyes, tears, darkness and night form an important body of 'hermetic' literature (hermetic, because specialists still debate the exact meaning of this curious literature). No wonder the popular theatre tended to send up these obscure inclinations, when so few understood their real nature.

John Dowland dedicated his *Second Booke of Songs*, (1600) to Lucy, and in it are found some of his darkest songs. The titles are like a roll-call of melancholy: 'I saw my Lady weep', 'Flow my tears'. 'Sorrow stay', 'Die not before thy day', 'Mourn, day is with darkness fled', is how the first five songs begin. Dowland is obviously complimenting Lucy and her 'school' of darkness, and is one of the chief architects of such a school. When more is known of this unusual lady, we may well be able to say that here is an equivalent to Ficino's academy patronised by Lorenzo de' Medici, in England – a hundred years later, led by a woman of stunning intelligence and beauty, who knew how to draw the best from her circle of artists and devotees.

Dowland was her chief musician, her high priest of melancholy. He was her Orpheus. So many of his powerful songs, supreme examples of inspired melancholy, are as though from the mouth of Orpheus in his self-imposed exile in the wilds of Thrace where for years, in isolation he bewailed his miserable condition. Curiously, Philomel, the nightingale, is the bird associated with Dowland (by Henry Peacham in his emblem-book *Minerva Brittana* of 1612) and was the only creature whom Orpheus addressed in his exile. Dowland consciously fashioned a melancholy, Orphic mask as his chief artistic persona and cultivated others to respond to his creation. Claimed by certain discerning contemporaries as such, Dowland became an incarnation of Orpheus, as Ficino had been a hundred years before.

Finally, in this general consideration of melancholy, we should spell out the true intention of this philosophy. The experienced paradox is that having listened to 'In darkness let me dwell' or any one of the other fourteen songs of darkness, the audience is not weighed down with black thoughts, or a surfeit of black bile, nor misery, nor suicide, but quite the reverse. The common exclamation is how refreshed one feels, lighter, more carefree, indeed, joyful. Revelation through catharsis is perhaps always seen as a journey through paradox. Certainly the outside observer is likely not to perceive the natural inner logic of such a charged experience.

Not every member of the audience is going to be profoundly moved or changed by melancholy music, nor will every reader of this book entirely agree with this proposal, there are after all twelve basic human personality types and there is always going to be at least one that experiences the opposite. I recall a recital of lute songs I was involved in at the Fitzwilliam Museum, Cambridge – a selection of fairly dolorous lyrics, typical of our choice at that time. The audience was small and specially invited, some event was being commemorated, and the atmosphere was highly charged. By the end of the one-hour performance there was something of 'an ecstatic transport' in the air. We felt quite pleased with this, but only to have any self-congratulatory praise shattered at the special reception afterwards, when the First Lady of the gathering said in a very precise and cutting upper-class English 'I preferred the pieces in the major key best'. Thinking over the song selection, it was clear what she intended – there was precisely one song in the major. So for her, any consideration of ecstatic transport was severely limited. Nevertheless I am sure that for most of the other members of the audience the catharsis through inspired melancholy was experienced in *some degree*, such that each person would, of course, have a different tale to tell and choose a different vocabulary to express it. Since it is not a fashionable mode of speech today few would speak of catharsis, Orphic influence, ecstatic transport or divine frenzy. In fact one reason why this book is necessary is that our language for communicating these experiences is very poorly developed, and by turning to the time of Ficino *et al.* we can borrow from an infinitely richer vocabulary to enrich our own. With the words come the ideas and understanding and clearer communication, without which we are left in the realm of nebulous entities. Oratory, after all, was one of Orpheus' skills, and is in rather a derelict state today.

THE ORPHIC SKILLS

What, precisely, are the skills associated with Orpheus? Can we be more precise about what constitutes 'Orphic'? It is not the nature of myth to be precise, for its meaning yields varying facets depending on the need of the searcher, but there are a series of constants which emerge regarding Orpheus which can be decorated and elaborated endlessly. The essential, archetypal (such an ugly word) Orpheus has four main roles:

(1) *the performer* – in oratory, poetry and music
(2) *the priest* – in ritual, revealing divine mysteries
(3) *the healer* – in restoring imbalance in body, mind and soul
(4) *the lover* – in drawing Eros to the world and so bringing harmony[5]

All these roles are intertwined, it is not that at one moment he turns priest or healer and stops being the performer or lover. The strands of his gifts each carry a divine furore which have, according to Ficino's observation, these appropriate effects. They:

(1)   calm the agitated soul
(2)   prepare the soul for exaltation
(3)   raise it up to the angelic level
(4)   unite it with the divine[6]

(Each number refers to the source number in the previous list of roles, yet also covers some aspects of the other three roles. For example, healing is involved in all four.) Ficino, as one inspired, tells how the performer making contact with his Orpheus, aroused by the Muses, will find that:

> His eyes burn, and he rises up on both feet and he knows how to sing tunes that he has never learnt.[7]

In this state of frenzy, the performer is able to transcend his normal limits, can perceive the mysteries of the Divine, and can present them to the audience in a manner which they will be able to understand. However, Ficino cautions that only Orpheus and King David had complete access to this exalted realm.

It is clear that contemplating Orpheus inspired Ficino and Dowland, but for us to appreciate the possibilities we need to be a little more familiar with his story and its interpretations.

There have been seven main phases of relating to the Orpheus mythology, which have included complete re-telling of the story without any regard for its original shape, size or meaning. Indeed surveying the seven periods brings home the fact that every age does violence to myth for its own ends, no doubt this book is no exception.[8]

The first stage is in the beginning when the myth was young and part of an unwritten oral tradition. It would seem that Orpheus, if ever such a person existed, was certainly pre-Homer, belonging in the second millennium BC – the Bronze Age. It is possible that he links with older Mycenaean origins and has vague connections with shamanistic practices relating to a Mother Goddess cult. But so misty is the origin, that only the fantasy can run riot with this 'first age' of Orpheus.

Any elaboration would be total fabrication. Nearest to this time is Homer's mention of Orpheus, as one of the crew of the 'Argonaut', along with Jason, in search of the Golden Fleece. But unlike the rest of the crew, Orpheus was never a soldier, did not do manly deeds, never killed or committed violence, and was eventually killed by women. All this sets him apart from the Greek pantheon of gods and men and leads to the saying that lyre players were weak and cowardly.

The second Orphic Age is better documented, yet some vital questions still remain unanswered. The Rome of Augustus saw a flowering of literature unparalleled in Roman history. (Within one generation there were Virgil, Ovid and Horace). The first full Orpheus story we have is found in Virgil's *Georgics* Book IV, where 75 lines are devoted to the myth by way of incidental reference, as an aside to a chapter on the merits and virtues of bee-keeping.[9] The handling of the story, though a literary masterpiece, suggests the author expects every reader to be already familiar with the outline and details so that he can make some changes to suit his own present purposes. Virgil was writing this in about 30BC, and only forty years later Ovid, in his *Metamorphoses* includes a wilfully adapted version of the Virgil telling.[10] Both poets are enjoying their literary virtuosity, and enjoying playing with their readers' oral tradition, so that it is difficult for us to know what belongs to the essential Orpheus and what is 'decadent' accretion of that Roman age.

The third age moves far further from the source, and unashamedly plays a part in the religious propaganda of the early Christians. In their efforts to combat the myriad of pagan cults that threatened to absorb Christianity, there was established, by scholars such as Clement of Alexandria, a body of literature which drew on pagan themes and emphasised their Christian possibilities. Orpheus was ideal material for Clement, where allegory became the paramount means of absorbing myth into church lore. Orpheus prefigured Christ, who rescued lost human souls in the form of Euridice.

Moving further still into fantasy is the fourth age of

Orpheus, embodied in Mediaeval Roman literature, where
Orpheus becomes the noble lover obeying the laws of the
troubador tradition and the art of courtly love. 'Sir Orfeo'
was a fourteenth century English poem based on an older
Breton ballad which fused classical, courtly love *and* celtic
mythology together.[11]

Towards the end of the fifteenth century, in the scholarly
hands of Marsilio Ficino, a new awareness of classical
sources was about. This fifth age of Orpheus is in many ways
the richest, not because of the discovery of new facts, though
anything new was absorbed into the Renaissance body of
knowledge, but because the figure of Orpheus was such a
direct inspiration on contemporary artists' work. In translat-
ing Plato, Orphic Hymns and the Corpus Hermeticum,
Ficino added commentary and gloss to the original works,
drawing out of these sources a new philosophy suffused with
the old. It was firmly believed that Orphic writings were of
great age, linking back to Orpheus himself, and only in the
seventeenth century was it discovered that there were late
compilations (second and third centuries AD) by various
mystery cults with an 'Orphic' outlook. For Ficino they carried
the pristine veracity of the master, and released into the
Renaissance awareness a strong dose of mystical doctrine that
inspired artists, poets, musicians for several generations.[12]

Orpheus, in his sixth age, becomes again a highly romanticised figure, a suitable legend for the 'pre-Raphaelite' school
to dwell on the agony of the separated lovers, or on Orpheus
as the first of all artists, alone in his inspiration.

In the last, and seventh age, Orpheus has been subjected to
an amazing variety of treatments. Wilfrid Mellers finds
endless inspiration in the agony and the ecstasy. In his writing
and even more in his lectures (where a veritable Augustinian
flood of rich rhetoric relives the Orphic dilemma) he pours his
enthusiasm into an erotic Orpheus of one's wildest dreams.[13]
Others, belonging more to a Behavioural school, consider
again the mode, morality and myth at work in the twentieth
century, whilst those of an archetypal persuasion wax

eloquent in obscure poems that do, indeed, touch our hearts. Yet others do immense service to the rest in their painstaking scholarship, such as in books like *Orpheus: the metamorphoses of a myth*, for example, by John Warden and his brethren (a major influence on the shaping of this present chapter). This seventh age sees a more diverse treatment of Orpheus than any other, where fact and fiction (three novels in 1988, released on Orpheus as a central figure) and mystery and self-knowledge all mix, harmoniously in the main, together.[14]

John Warden, in his opening editorial, says that 'myth is the currency in which our culture is transmitted'. Since matters pertaining to Orpheus have been retold for four thousand years, we should have a quick look at this currency. Here follows a digest, as I see it, of the salient points of the Orpheus material. For a fuller account, the reader is recommended Warden's anthology.

THE MYTH OF ORPHEUS

The original myth is lost, and there are variations to every part of the story, and some parts appeal to one more than another. Orpheus was born of the union of Apollo, the Sun god, and Calliope, the Muse of Epic Poetry and Eloquence. He was therefore familiar with the higher slopes of Parnassus from birth. He was destined to be a performer. Hermes had invented the lyre in an idle playful moment, but though a toy, it was the toy of a god. Hermes gave it to Apollo, who was flattered by it, and also gave it to Orpheus, who was thus empowered directly by the gods to communicate divine inspiration through his singing and playing.

Orpheus travelled in the Argonaut with Jason to recover the Golden Fleece from Colchis. He took no part in masculine prowess, or show of arms. He was regarded as a singer, a player of the lyre, a prophet, a shaman, a magician. He was also a lover.

As well as a lover of things divine, he loved the young

nymph, Euridice. Their mutual love became an emblem of faithfulness. Euridice died from a snakebite on the heel (several different stories tell of how this came about) and was taken down into Hades.

Orpheus was beside himself with grief and determined to enter Hades to find her and bring her back to the world. He gained access to Hades, normally closed to living mortals, by his powers of persuasion in speech and song. To Pluto and Persephone he sang a lament which touched Persephone's heart thus persuading Pluto to release Euridice. There was one taboo placed on this decree: that Orpheus must trust she was following him, and not look back until they had returned to the world.

Fatefully, at the last moment of the ascent, Orpheus faltered and turned, only to see Euridice already becoming a wraith, a soundless word of lament on her lips. Orpheus, desperate in his anguish, attempted to descend to Hades again, but no persuasion would allow a second entrance. Distraught, he abandoned society and retired to the rocky wilderness of northern Thrace where he sang endlessly his inconsolable lament. His howling was heard only by one nightingale, who was profoundly inspired by his song, and imitated it. Other wild animals became tamed by his singing. For years Orpheus dwelt in this distracted condition, hating all women. Some Bacchantes, female followers of Dionysus, heard his wail and became angry at his misogyny and tore him apart, limb by limb. His severed head and lyre were thrown into the River Hebrus, floated down into the Aegean Sea, and eventually carried into the barren shores of the island Lesbos. All this time the head continued to wail its plangent song. The lyre was returned to Apollo, and the head continued to give oracles even though buried, until Apollo decreed that no more oracles would be given by the head. The silence that followed gave rise, over centuries, to a growing body of written and oral material that purported to be by Orpheus.

'The Rhapsodic Theogony' is ascribed to Orpheus, by ancient tradition, and forms a central body of material of a particularly bizarre kind. Essentially primitive images are woven into a sophisticated web telling a complex story of creation according to Orpheus.

It leads from Chronos (Time) creating the world out of water and primeval ooze, and after many sensational twists and turns ends with the creation of mankind from the ashes of Titans who had been destroyed by Zeus for destroying his son Dionysus. Dionysus was re-made from his heart, saved by Athena, and mankind was made from elements of ashes and Dionysus. This twofold nature (representing Heaven and Earth) caused man's fundamental conflict – he wished to partake of things divine, yet was held back, by his earthly body. The Way of Orpheus was, through asceticism, ritual, and purification, to purge the Titanic ashes and become wholly divine. The body is evil and soiled and forms a tomb for the soul (echoed in Dowland's 'In darkness let me dwell'), and only with the death of the body can the Orphic initiate join with its higher nature. Through thousand-year cycles of re-birth men must become purified. The Orpheus cult is the antithesis of all other Greek religions.

There, in outline, is the myth of Orpheus and the central cult that became attached to his name. I have avoided many details of the story, and numerous variants, and the Orphic cult is far richer and more varied than I have suggested here. But this provides a basis on which I can elaborate for the purposes of this chapter.[15]

THE SIGNIFICANCE OF ORPHEUS

As I have suggested, everyone approaching the story has used it for their own coloured interpretations. I propose to do exactly the same, but will consider what some others have proposed before. Some early versions of the story had Orpheus being successful in returning Euridice to the living world, and this of course alters the possible symbolism in a rather vital way. By contrast Boethius, in his *Consolation of Philosophy* depicted Euridice as being the heavy bonds of

Earth dragging the soul (Orpheus) downwards. His ascent from Hell, without her, was his triumph, and he then sang songs of joy of the released spirit. In an early version the nymph was called Agriope, which means the 'savage watcher', whereas 'Euridice' means a 'wide path'. Both names are associated with the Queen of the Night, Persephone, and Orpheus has been known to take her hand and steal her from the King of the Night, Pluto.

The name 'Orpheus' means 'skilful' or 'artful', and most commentators seem to agree on that fairly obvious etymology. As for the general point of the myth, most have considered it broadly to mean the advance of civilisation, through art, against the forces of violence and savagery, not only a taming, but also a refining. The descent of Euridice into Hell has been seen as the descent of the soul into the body (the body *is* Hell) and Orpheus represents divine powers which come to reclaim the soul. If every performer has an Orpheus within, then it seems fruitful to consider that every audience contains Euridice. The performance is itself the descent, where lovers meet and recognise each other, take hands and ascend, united, together. The culmination, the distilled silence at the end of a work, or recital, is heaven. Sometimes the ascent succeeds, sometimes, even at the last moment, the Orpheus in the performer may doubt, and the final union is lost. Thus both versions of the ancient myth are re-enacted in performance but success is not possible without Orpheus and Euridice working together.

This reading of the story, charging ordinary performance with legendary powers and inviting Love to attend the event brings us close to one aspect of the core of Orphic material so dear to the Medici neo-Platonists. Another description of creation later than that found in the *Rhapsodic Theogony*, is described by Plato: the first manifestation of creation was utter chaos, for the four elements – Earth, Water, Air and Fire – were in confusion, as though at war, for none knew their rightful place in the order of creation. Love (Eros) descended and showed each its proper quarter, gave each its self-respect, and harmonised the whole. Love thus created order out of chaos, thus a harmonious continuation can be maintained. One of the lyrics of Ben Jonson, set by Alfonso Ferrabosco, states the process superbly, setting in motion a proportioned, cosmological dance:

> So Beauty on the waters stood,
> When Love had severed earth from flood.
> So when he parted air from fire,
> He did with concord all inspire.
> And then a motion he them taught
> That elder than himself was thought;
> Which thought was yet the child of earth,
> For Love is elder than his birth.[16]

Eros is one of the most ancient of the gods in Orphic theogony. In some aspects, he was the first creation of Chronos, being one manifestation of Phanes ('who held swift and blind Love dear in his heart'), when he emerged out of the silvery egg created by Chronos in the ether. For the song to say he is 'elder than his birth' refers to this creation myth. Ficino's translation of Plato says of Love that he is ancient and 'self-perfecting', and Warden's gloss on Ficino says 'the object created completes its own creation by turning, in its love, to its creator' (p. 79). Orphic songs, for Ficino, manifest the descent of Love. The diagram overleaf reveals the dance which Love sets in motion.

Hermes, the messenger of the gods to men, the thrice greatest, the revealer of mysteries, presented his divine toy, the lyre, first to Apollo, then to Orpheus, who is the first poet to celebrate divine mysteries in his verse. This gift came directly from Hermes, along with the lyre, and a lineage was created which from a Renaissance point of view went like this: Apollo; Orpheus; Pythagoras; Plato; Ficino; Dowland (with the last name being whoever was regarded as closest to the Orphic spirit in whichever company or circle you were in). An added eccentricity was the need to weave into this essentially pagan lineage the figure of the psalm-singing King

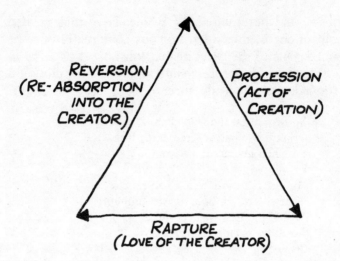

Figure 12

David. It was agreed that he should be in there somewhere, but the position varied – Ficino was inclined to place him alongside Orpheus, so that the Christian pedigree could match the pagan one – each recipient having it straight from the Divine. The lyre (or harp for David) was passed, symbolically speaking, to the next in line. The lyre itself, made from the shell of a tortoise, with the horns of a bull, the hide of a cow and strings of sheeps-gut was also invested with divine power (because made by the hands of Hermes). The parts of the animals that made it up were sacrificed for the advancement of culture (sufficient redress for the guts of the tortoise being torn out?). The instrument represented the harmony of the spheres ('as above, so below', with Hermes the mediator) and its seven strings represented the law of number governing the structure of the universe, which knowledge was made available by Pythagoras, proving he was in line with a divine plan. (A note is hardly necessary, but may clear up some confusion: the Renaissance period fully understood the nature of the Orphic lyre, but made no attempt to build an instrument exactly like it in construction. Leonardo is known to have created a special instrument, made from a horse's skull, covered in silver and roughly harplike in its musical functioning (this was for a special masque created for the Sforza household). Otherwise, two instruments served the function of the lyre. The one favoured by Ficino was the lire (the term he used, but actually a generic term in fifteenth century Italian for any kind of string instrument) which was actually a 'lira da braccio', a stringed bowed instrument held at the shoulder (like the violin) with one or two 'bordon' strings running off the fingerboard which acted as drones, or could be plucked by the thumb of the left hand, which otherwise held the neck of the instrument. The fingers of that hand stopped the strings to provide simple harmonies for relatively simple melodies. Always this is the instrument Ficino used to accompany his chanting. Otherwise, the most common instrument, throughout the Renaissance, which did duty for the Orphic lyre was the lute, which is now so well known because of the early music revival as not to need detailed description here. Sufficient to say that the symbolic lore attached to the lute, its proportions, the rose design, the strings, the intervals, makes it a suitable substitute symbolically speaking. It had the advantage over the 'lira da braccio' that it could achieve much more complex music, and was therefore attractive to the great performers of that time – Ficino was a musical philosopher, but Dowland was a philosophising musician.)

Most of the foregoing material has inevitably been concerned with establishing a picture, or series of reference points on the 'Orpheus without'. Now we must turn 180°, as it were, and consider the 'Orpheus within'. A shifting set of mythological stories, a changing historical set of interpretations to suit the time or purpose, a rag-bag of mystical writings by unknown seers – armed with this equipment we turn to see if there *is* an Orpheus within to respond to our search, to ask, indeed, 'Is there anyone there?'

Marsilio Ficino again provides us with the most useful and inspiring material. He tells us:

The direction to Truth lies through contemplation (introspection), so that the mind-space becomes more and more like that of the Divine Mind in relation to his creation.[17]

The present contemplation focusses on music and the soul, and is a fusion of material presented by Warden from Ficino's work, with Plato and Orphic fragments, added to which is my own position as a performing artist. It is, in other words, a synthesis of some of the most exciting material ever set down as a guide for the performer.

DIVINE MUSIC

As we read in Ficino's letter (quoted on page 14) there are two kinds of divine music, not heard by us at all – there is the silent music contained entirely in the Divine mind, and then the heavenly music of the spheres, created by the movement of the planets as they make their cosmic dance. Apparently this noise of creation in movement is so unbelievably loud that we cannot hear it. It is also, we are told, incredibly beautiful, beyond imagining.

The 'idea' of the divine music is imprinted in the human soul, which is the only way we could understand something which is beyond our senses. The reflection of the divine music manifests at every level of our existence; through reason, imagination, discourse, song, instrumental music, in dance. This outward and downward movement through the levels of human existence is experienced, and explored in the work of all artists: orators, poets, musicians, painters, sculptors, and architects. All arts are moved by this divine music, are a reflection and an embodiment of it.

Men and women also have two types of music: the music held in mind, which is the concept of order and harmony expressed in sound – a 'speculative' music; and the music as expressed in performance in song, instrumental play, and dance. The second, to be in good shape, must be ordered by the first. The problem is, we get so caught in the *activity* of making music and the many practical problems it poses, that we forget to exercise the first music, the music of the mind.

The performance of music (which includes singing and playing) starts from the mind, the imagination and the heart of the performer. This volition is then expressed in movement and activity, which causes vibration, sound. These impulses travel on the air and strike the *spiritus* of the listener. The *spiritus* is also composed of air, so that like meets like, recognises it, and 'receives' it, that is, takes it in. So then, once received, these impulses are translated back into the language of the heart, imagination and inner mind of the listener. (Ficino's words confirm our diagram of the energy flow described on page 45).

The central 'nub' of this communication rests on the exact nature of *spiritus*. Robert Jones, in his preface (p. 15) says of the senses that 'they are the soules Intelligencers', and that the ear is the best tuned 'so spirituall, that it catcheth up wilde soundes in the Aire, and bringes them under a government'. Jones is an informed neo-Platonist, for the established doctrine sees the spirit as the 'nodus' of soul and body, that is, the point where the physical world meets with the subtle world, or world of soul.

Human spirit occupies this central position *animus – spiritus – corpus*, and holds together the two outer utterly-unlike substances. Spirit is the 'interface' which allows the parts of the human being to operate. Its nature is of a fine and transparent vapour, generated from the subtle blood (found near the heart) and, through the heat of the heart, the vaporisation continues. (Is it necessary at this point to caution the reader in order not to confuse 'objective medicine' as we know it today and 'subjective medicine' as it is being used here in order to understand a subtle mechanism for which modern practice has no observation at all? In this context the 'idea' or 'concept' is of more value than the matter). Because the spirit is an airy vapour, it is nourished by things of that element, particularly sweet sounds of concord. The performing arts of music and poetry were very highly regarded precisely for this reason, namely, to feed the spirit.

Ficino and Plato then move from the consideration of human spirit to the contemplation of world spirit. (Again these 'ideas' are a little strange when measured against what we now know of the physical universe, especially the structure and functioning of the solar system, yet there is still something of their 'subjective' approach which has not been invalidated. Reading the closing sentences of Stephen Hawking's *A Brief History of Time* is almost like reading undiluted Ficino!)[18]

Creation is divided into two portions. Below the Moon the physical universe is manifest, and subject to the laws of Nature and Time. Above the Moon, are the Heavens, filled with wheeling planets, choirs of Angels, Intelligences, etc. God looks down on this entire creation. Joining the physical universe to the heavens is the world-spirit, which penetrates every part of creation, descending from God, energised by him, and linking up from the highest to the lowest. It is an uninterrupted current of supernatural energy forming a *circuitus spiritualis*, moving forever down and back. The entire hierarchy of creation is dependent on its every moment.

In John Warden's words, the aim of 'the musician is to plug into this current'. If the human spirit can be drawn into precise alignment, or oneness with the world-spirit and thus increase the energy available, the awareness of performer and audience will move on to a higher, more refined level of consciousness. The Orpheus within will have drawn the influence of the gods directly into our sphere of experience. We cease to be as wild beasts, ferocious and unruly, and become civilised. We are truly 'educated', led from the dark to the light, Euridice and Orpheus bound by golden chains of Love.

The question now is, to whom or what is the performance being addressed? To the audience, yes, on one level, even the performer to himself, a necessary dialogue, but there is a suggestion, in that we 'will have drawn the influence of the gods directly into our sphere', of addressing the gods directly, of aiming a little higher. Ficino gets very excited, and spends many pages on the need to address, in the appropriate manner, astral deities in order to attract down their rich influences. This is astral magic, make no mistake, and was a hot and dangerous subject around 1490.[19] How Ficino got away with it reflects, in some measure, the skill he had in drawing down powerful influences!

Ficino lists the astral deities, the kind of appropriate scents, colours, moods, modes, times of day, season, etc. Much of this information he took directly from the introductions to the Orphic Hymns, but a great deal was also added from the general 'law of correspondences' which maintained general currency throughout the sixteenth and part of the seventeenth century. This law drew parallels from every level of the hierarchy of creation, so that a rose, a lion, an eagle corresponded to each other in that they were the finest or highest example of their particular level of creation.[20] They were therefore fit emblems for a king or emperor. This is a very simple outline of 'the law of correspondences' which was worked out in immense length and staggering complexity. Ficino enhanced his creation of an appropriate ambience for addressing the deities by calling on this convention.

A strong sense of ritual pervades all this thinking. In one Orphic text, Orpheus promises to teach his pupil Museus the proper rites in relation to the singing of the hymns. Ficino is meticulous about detail, yet leaves us with some unfortunate gaps, such as exactly *what* music to play on these occasions.

The deity most often called upon by Ficino is Apollo, the Sun god and the father of Orpheus. The invocation of Apollo follows Plato's belief that the sun was the visible offspring of God, and it is Apollo who leads the other deities in the daily heavenly dance to God. In invoking the sun the supplicant is more than attempting to draw down solar influence but it is an attempt for the soul to be drawn to more profound understanding of God. Ficino encapsulates the situation boldly: nature offers a set of signs and symbols; the mind needs comparative study; the soul needs magic. This simple equation is expanded: we discuss the *nature* of the sun, because we can see it in nature but we are really discussing the *nature of God*, which cannot be observed directly. However, in the very process of communication (or communing) we partake of the essential mystery.

Although Ficino believed in the efficacy of hymnsinging (with all appropriate ritual and qualities being observed), and with this action communicated with the deities and attracted down their powers into us, his own teacher, Germistos Plethon, held a more circumspect point of view. He believed that hymnsinging, and all the rest, moulded the mind and imagination of the celebrants so that they were able, by these practices, to consider and contemplate higher things. The difference is of some importance, for Plethon comes over as a more modern, psychologically aware mind. Certainly there is less resistance generally to the idea of 'mind-improvement' than there might be to the pouring down of stellar magic into the recipient. Although, in performance, some very strange things can happen, and it may be as well to keep an open mind.

CHAPTER SIX

Concepts at work

FACE to face with the essential nature of 'performance' and seeing a 'portrait' of the inner Orpheus suggests it is perhaps time to draw breath for a moment and consider where we now stand.

The neo-Platonic working model described in the last chapter may take some swallowing, not least because twentieth century science denies the physical possibility of such a model. *Spiritus* is not something which can be weighed, measured or in any way directly observed, and yet a number of readers will feel, along with me, that 'there is *something* in it'. Not least it has the value of being a harmonious creation of the mind which *might* be possible, stretching known physical laws a little; it gives a creative direction to follow; does no one any harm. And most curious of all, it seems to work! As a hypothesis for the inner nature, function and purpose of performance, it will serve until an equally profound but more precisely observed model is presented.

In this chapter I want to take a series of points arising from the last, examine them a little more closely and present some practical examples of the concepts at work. These are all autobiographical, not because of a desire to be self-centred, but because precise observation of performance as it unfolds is essential. First-hand experience, at this point, is needed to balance four thousand years of myth-making.

Ficino described dramatically the feeling when Orpheus steps upward and outward from within you, and uses you to sing songs you have never learned. This experience can be terrifying at the time, indeed often the moment before he is about to step out we fasten down the hatches, keep him inside and take a safer route through. The times when Orpheus stands forward, noble and free, pouring forth songs, words or tunes you have never heard are times one can remember. These are times when concern for *decoro* or *sprezzatura* disappear – you find the truth is being spoken through you, despite yourself. 'Truth' is actually a very ancient creation, for she is the only daughter of 'Time' (you may remember *Chronos* creating the world out of water and ooze; he also begat 'Truth', she is perennially youthful and innocent).

TEMENOS

As Orpheus steps forward a new quality, or dimension, takes the stage, which feels like stepping into another reality. This, in my experience, is witnessed as much by the audience as the performer. The new space is *temenos*, an ancient Greek word for an ancient concept – a sacred space, often in the enclosure of a temple, in which sacred arts are performed with dignity and appropriate ritual. With the creation of *temenos*, the performance that follows takes a different set of dimensions. Every action has space around it; every body has a spacious aura, making each performer seem larger than life; whatever the physical lighting before, there is now a special lucency which illuminates the space. Sound qualities change, so that there is a limpid clarity to the voice or music. Time takes a different pace, as though every detail might take a delightful eternity. These are all signs that *temenos* has been marked out.

I find the concept of *temenos* wonderfully exciting, but is it really possible in the mundane experience? Well, resoundingly, yes! For a number of years I have had occasion to return to Dartington, in Devon, England, usually for the annual summer school which takes place in August. First, twenty-five years ago, I went as a student; recently I have returned as a performer, teacher, director. I recall in the first visits the experience of sitting in the Great Hall, listening to some of the finest performers at work, and being profoundly moved, again and again, by performances of all kinds – music normally quite outside my sphere of interest. That hall so often has a blessed quality, but not always. It is not something which can be guaranteed. In recent years I have been on the other side of the platform, and experienced the incredible charge of energy invested in that space. Last year, I was about to enter the hall with Evelyn Tubb to present a recital called 'Heaven and Earth' – devotional and erotic songs from Dowland to Purcell. In the few minutes before going on, Evelyn was practising her 'tai chi' (a wonderful technique for performance preparation, incidentally) and I was idly looking over notices and leaflets about future events at Dartington. Coming up in November was the annual seminar of *Temenos*, the journal begun and nurtured by Kathleen Raine. I had contributed a small article to the second issue of that journal, had promised several times to produce another, and regretted not being free for the seminar. The leaflet outlined, in the most poetic prose, precisely the concept of *temenos* and the appropriateness of Dartington as a venue for such a gathering. Reading this focussed twenty-five years' experiences in the Great Hall. Here, for me, was a perfect example of *temenos* at work, and the very time-span of my experience gave it something of a feeling of 'tradition'. I was about to enter that special space once again, after the lapse of one year, to an audience who in large part were also returning. Something special was needed.

No one though was ready for the next step; as Evelyn and I entered the Hall to enthusiastic applause full of expectancy, Evelyn slipped on the uneven polished oak planks, and almost fell to the ground with her part-book thrown to the floor. The audience gasped for breath, whilst still applauding, almost cried out in support and goodwill, sighed with relief when Evelyn righted herself, and then there was a silence so

intense. All this took a moment. Then I had to stand forward
and speak. Any plans I had made to outline the programme
theme had been scattered with Evelyn's part-book, my mind
had seized up, and yet there I was standing forward in that
immense silence. Fortunately Orpheus stepped forward, and
spoke through me, making first a light little joke about
Evelyn's stability, and then moved straight into speaking of
temenos and the sacred space of Dartington Great Hall, the
annual ritual of returning, and eventually to the inspiration
for this programme – 'as above, so below'. I have no idea of
the words that were used, only the most general outline that I
have given here. But throughout the week that followed
people sought me out to say how much they enjoyed the
recital but *particularly* the special words at the beginning.
Incidentally, Orpheus speaking gave Evelyn time to recover
her normal composure, and when we were ready for the first
song ('In this trembling shadow' as it happened!) she performed as though nothing had gone wrong. The concept of
temenos elaborated a powerful ritual in which the entire
gathering took part, everything was harmoniously balanced,
the light had a golden aura, we were bathed in Love.

The Great Hall at Dartington is a special place, and a
sceptic might say that my description is a highly romanticised
version because of my natural liking for mediaeval structures,
or might put it down to my very genuine admiration for the
founders' ambitions which set the Dartington experiment in
motion. Both things are certainly true, but I quote another
example which could not claim any such special qualities.
Emma Kirkby and I were to give a one-hour Sunday afternoon recital for a music society linked with IBM in their very
splendid mansion south of London. We drove out of town in
time for a brief rehearsal, for we knew the programme very
well, and arrived at the place in good time. The imposing
portals of the eighteenth century mansion beckoned and we
attempted our entrance. The entire place was locked, sealed,
burglar-alarmed and clearly shut for the weekend. We discovered after some time and exhaustive enquiries that the

recital was not in the mansion but in a small, temporary prefabricated hut in another part of the grounds. These buildings did duty for a number of various conflicting events (it was an all-purpose social centre for IBM employees), including badminton, TV room, showers, kitchen and a small hall of truly dreadful dimensions. The platform set up for us appeared to be a series of up-turned beer crates covered in some undistinguished cloth – the whole thing rocked as one moved about on it. The ceiling was low, the walls were part-curtained (absorbing what little resonance there might have been) and along the back wall was an open passageway for the healthy white-shorts brigade (off to play badminton), forming a steady flow of traffic.

We rehearsed for three or four minutes and gave up, in despair. The sound seemed to travel about three feet, then drop heavily to the floor. We had never been in a place with such appalling acoustics as these. The audience began to arrive, and were clearly very eager, and so we consoled ourselves with the fact that their enthusiasm would make up for the dreadful sound. Half an hour later we teetered on to the rocking platform, bowed, sat and waited for silence. This meant comparative silence, for the game of badminton could be heard next door. But our audience was incredible, for they, not in the least bit distracted, focussed their entire attention on us. We began to play, and wonder of wonders, the acoustics were clear and clean, quite transformed. Now by the laws of physics, eighty bodies in that small room should have absorbed any vestige of acoustics that were left, but instead the *quality of the audience's attention* turned it into a place with a certain beauty of sound. So eagerly had they awaited this recital, such enthusiasm was in the air that *temenos* was created so obviously that the sourest sceptic would have been won over. The occasion lives in our memories, and for at least some in the audience too, for we met two of them recently when I used this example in a lecture and they, unsolicited, confirmed that this experience took place.

I want to turn now to Ficino's concern to address the astral deities in appropriate manner, so as to infuse the performer, and via him the audience, with the qualities invested. How can this be translated into practical action for today? I remind the reader of Plethon's difference of emphasis, rather a moulding of the mind and imagination towards the desired influence, than a bringing down of heavenly vibrations. Does it matter which? Not much really, providing we use it creatively. The ideas are themselves an inspiration. Ficino had an almost obsessive concern for Apollo, perhaps unconsciously correcting a personal inclination of his towards a heavy saturnine outlook (excess of melancholy brought about by an over-zealous studiousness, so he diagnosed for himself).

Every age sounds a different tone, operates in a different mode, and responds to a different combination of influences. If for Ficino's time Apollo was the central reference point, it is quite possible that today we may need a different orientation. Strong contenders would include Eros, Venus, Hermes, the Muses, Dionysus, and even Pan and forgotten lower deities of the forest. All of these would act as balances or correctives to modern inclinations: to an over-mechanised society and excessive urbanisation. Imagine the *panic* and *pandemonium* if the Arts Council were to give grants for the quality of projects relating to Pan! Strange to say, but I think a new awakening to some of these deities and their attributes would bring about a new *humanising* of the arts, and would spin off an increased spate of creativity.

Witness the extraordinary burst of music-theatre in the seventeenth century, released through a new desire to identify the gods, goddesses, demons, and their interference in or aid to human affairs. The *deux ex machina* literally brought down not only the influence of the gods, but actors and actresses standing in for them. For a hundred years many of the operas, masques and ballets concerned themselves with divine manifestations of one sort or another. Admittedly this is a bit down-market from what Ficino had in mind, but the desire and process of making manifest divine attributes is very much the same. Anyone who has witnessed a production of one of these spectacles will know of the theatrical, indeed magical, power that is communicated. In my own experience, the nearest I have got to such material was in a student production of Matthew Locke's enormous spectacle, *Psyche* (1675). The original ran for over four hours, had a cast of over 120, and was a 'Broadway' success in its day. Our reduced version ran for a mere three hours without an interval, and was a powerful experience, at least for most of those involved. The work swings very much on the interference of the gods in human affairs, the central action being Cupid falling in love with Psyche. Although the production has many precursors of English pantomime (two men play the ugly sisters; Cupid, the principal boy, is played by a girl; Psyche is an early version of Cinders, etc.), and therefore uses comedy to a considerable extent, the undertones of the work are decidedly serious. Even in this student production, several scenes live in the mind for their incredible dramatic, magical power of a kind described by Ficino. For example in the palace of Cupid, all the statues come alive and dance, then return to statues again; the demonic power of ten furies as they sing their bizarre polyphony, driving the ugly sister into Hell; the ritualistic priests of Apollo scene, where the oracle of Apollo speaks the fateful curse on Psyche. Over and over again the work uses ritual and magic for its theatrical effect, but perhaps the finest moment is the seemingly simple scene when Cupid and Psyche first acknowledge, then kiss and consummate their love, in a sequence of sensuous, yet platonic beauty, enhanced by the play of sexuality (Cupid played by a girl). So many forgotten works of the seventeenth century remain to be rediscovered today. If we attempt the production techniques and lighting of that time, we may well witness a re-birth of the deities on earth, at least in the safe confines of theatre. By so doing we will release something of the enhancement of spirit so sought after by Ficino in his Apollonian, Orphic-inspired hymn singing.

It certainly is not necessary though for a performance to attempt a thorough re-invoking of seventeenth century spectacle. In any case this is, in fact impossible to every detail. Backstage machinery, rush lighting, sumptuous costume, exquisite sets, months of rehearsal – the finance is simply not available, for now society spends on film extravaganzas rather than millions on one-off live events. Occasional glimpses into the exotic world of seventeenth century music-theatre will have to suffice, but the simplest of means can create the most profound transformations.

The woodcut of the Orphic hymnsinging, with one sole performer singing to the 'lira-da-braccio' is much easier to recreate (p. 7). What is more important than resembling the outer show of performance is the aim for authenticity of spirit – a lead given us by the Renaissance practice of using a lute or lira-de-braccio instead of a lyre. Programme planning can be of fundamental importance in this regard. If the hidden design of a programme is based on sound principles, if it clothes essential concepts, then the audience will enjoy the benefit of that clarity of thought, even if the construction details are not revealed to them. A performance must become more than a mere musical (or balletic, or theatrical) experience if the powers of Orpheus are to be invoked. It must tell a story, which contains fundamental truths, it must enhance the concept of *musica speculativa* in its widest sense, so that the programme intention or design itself reflects the divine music. Otherwise a delightful entertainment can be had by all and – Poof! Gone in a moment!

This means in practice learning to work with the languages of myth and symbol; of refining the understanding of archetypal interplay; of learning to use numerology as a creative design tool; of realising the theatrical dimension of the performing space, so that even the violinist realises he is an actor in that space; to develop an appropriate use of ritual, (perhaps even so that it is not noticed as such by the auditors), so that *temenos* is strengthened.

I offer two contrasting examples from my own experience

where attention to these matters has really paid off. The first is of the simplest, close to Ficino's heart I would think. Emma and I have for a number of years performed a one-hour lute song programme on the theme of the effect of time on human affairs, on the concept of all below the moon being subject to change and decay. Edmund Spenser's *Mutabilitie Cantos* set the scene in the printed programme:

> What man that sees the ever-whirling wheels
> Of Change, the which all mortal things doth sway,
> But that thereby doth find and plainly feele
> How Mutability in them doth play
> Her cruell sports, to many men's decay?

We gave the programme the title 'Time Stands Still' from the song of that name by John Dowland. This was the last of twelve lyrics presented in the programme, a profound contemplation which somehow achieves the claim of its first line. Before that there were eleven different ways of considering the effect of time on human experience. The theme is simple, yet rich; it addresses everyone in the audience, young and old immediately; the ideas are perennial yet clothed in some of the finest lyric poetry in our language. The proportion, based on numerological thinking, worked as a perfect balance and the means to realise it were of the simplest – a voice and a lute alone. The printed programme contained the Spenser cantos, a brief introduction to the essential ideas of change and metamorphosis, and the twelve lyrics, so that the listener would take away the ideas for later contemplation. There is enough food for thought in that poetry to last many years. Rarely have performances of this recital been less than magical because of the beauty of the matter, the harmony of the design, and its relevance to the audience.

The second example was on an altogether different scale: it was a one-off event held at the South Bank in the summer of 1988, designed to celebrate Midsummer's Night, and was called 'The Revels of Siena'. It was an 'all-niter' which ran from 11.00 pm with foyer events through to breakfast of *pro-*

secco and *panino* on the terrace at 8.00 am. There were eight hours' non-stop music and theatre through the night. Almost a hundred people took part in the performance until the finale, when the entire audience joined in a kind of Renaissance conga and danced out to breakfast. Close on a thousand people witnessed this event, which was sheer good fun from beginning to end.

So what has this to do with Ficino and Orpheus? Behind the atmosphere of revels and carefree enjoyment was a design and concept that would certainly have appealed to those savants of divine frenzy. The event was, essentially, a *bacchanalia* addressed to Dionysus. Seven times through the night the powers of night were invoked, a mystic ritual indeed, and seven times the listener was invited to sweet reverie. Sleep was invited, but the invitation was accepted by very few, rather the chain of events drew us into an ever more alert state – as though becoming drunk on polyphony, getting high but the senses becoming clearer. There was definitely a strong pagan flavour to the night, but none of the forces were frightening, quite the reverse. Walking amongst the breakfast-time picknickers was an extraordinary experience (we were blessed with a wonderful warm sunny Sunday morning on the terrace, probably the only one of the year). We all knew we had been through something unique, but out in the sunshine it was already receding into night-time fantasy – it was, literally, a mid-summer night's dream. Yet we were touched by something incredibly powerful through the night, and meeting those who took part months later they became almost incandescent with golden memories. The final deity was decidedly Apollonian, via a beautiful evoking of Aurora, but joining everyone together was Eros. Throughout the night Hermes had been very active, and played a number of tricks, and the Muses were certainly in attendance. All the deities could only function however because of a very skilful backstage team of humans whose virtuoso display of administration went by unnoticed, but was enjoyed by everyone. Holding the whole in place, however, – the united audience, the inspired performers, the brilliant organisation, the presence of the gods – was the concept, the very ancient tradition of recognising mid-summer as a turning-point of the year and taking part in that wonderful dance.

TRANSFORMATION

I would like to make a detailed examination of how these changes in consciousness come about in performance, by taking a very particular example. In 1613 there was published *The Songs of Mourning*,[1] a funeral elegy lamenting the death of Prince Henry, the next in line for the throne after King James, and because of his untimely death at the age of 18, followed by his younger brother Charles. Henry had been a focal point, an emblem, for all future hopes in the arts – poets, musicians, painters, architects gathered at his court (although he was only eighteen) and created a circle of extraordinary creativity. Henry was seen as an embodiment of divine power, with great personal skills and discrimination – a future patron of the highest quality. His early death was, therefore, a blow of the greatest magnitude. Many kinds of elegies poured forth which expressed in more or less formal language the true desolation felt by many. The arts were bereft of one of their greatest protectors.

The Songs of Mourning was a collection of seven poems written by Thomas Campion, who was not only a poet to Prince Henry, but one of his chief physicians as well, and thus very close to the Prince right until the end. The music was by John Coprario, music tutor to the Prince and one of the great innovators in English music at that time. The song-cycle, one of the first genuine cycles in the English language, had a number of functions. One was to express, in formal terms, the loss to the two artists who owed Henry so much; another was to assuage the grief of the court circle through performance of this cycle as a kind of artistic ritual; yet a third, because of the nature of the dedication of each of the songs to a member of the royal household, was to ease the bereavement of those members. Fourth was to open out the address to the listening world so that they might pay their respects to the departed; next, by expressions of grief, the very grief may become spent so that the delayed marriage celebrations of Henry's sister, Elizabeth, to the Count Palatine of the Rhine, Frederick the Fifth, might take place without undue delay. By opening up the wound of grief, by 'bleeding' it with this elegy, Charles may be prepared more quickly to take his bold brother's place. And lastly, by the right expression of grief, in poetry, music and performance, the departed soul of Henry might be able to wing its way heavenward with more ease, leaving these songs transmitted on the ether.

Some of this seems far-fetched to a modern mind, yet assuredly this is the line of thinking belonging to the time of composing. Catharsis appropriate to several levels of appreciation was considered to operate. But how can a work written to meet such a specific need almost four hundred years ago have any relevance or power in performance now? How does something so specific translate into a very different society?

Emma and I have performed the work on a number of occasions and have had the chance to observe in some detail the means of transformation, for that, essentially, is what happens to everyone witnessing the unfolding of the cycle in the twenty-five minutes it takes. It is a guided meditation – guided because the route for the mind is plotted out in very great detail, every stage of the meditational journey is pre-set. Armed with a copy of the words and their individual dedications, I begin the performance with an improvised introduction, setting the scene. Prince Henry needs a few words, so that his position and importance is established; the whole nation in mourning establishes a general elegiac mood; then a brief discussion of the structure of the elegy and an introduction to the lesser-known dedicatees. In conclusion, the whole is described as a series of 'veils' of grief. As a song is concluded, the listener is lifted up out of that layer of grief and as it were, cleansed of it. That layer of grief is removed by its very expression. In due measure, in a focussed silence the work then begins. The genius of Campion and Coprario is immediately apparent, they have succeeded, in some manner, to encapsulate the character or position of each dedicatee: regal, formal and stately for James; regal, feminine and more intimate for Anne; resolute, bold yet respectful for Charles; incredibly delicate, gentle and the epitome of femininity for his sister Elizabeth; friendship, brothers-in-arms and through marriage, stoic for Frederick; more formal and distant for Great Britain; and finally the apotheosis of a distant deity for the World.

How Campion and Coprario achieve this subtle shift of emphasis is miraculous. One can point, in the poetry, to Campion's use of various different line-lengths, verse forms, the dissonance and assonance of particular vocabulary; or in Coprario's variety of rhythms, musical word stress, speed of harmonic change, or unexpected melodic intervals – study can yield much to suggest how the two achieved variety, but the overall unity of purpose defies analysis. The listener takes the whole step by step, and to some degree takes on the character, or listens from a similar position to that of the dedicatee. Internally, during the process of guided meditation, an appropriate stance is taken up. This may be, foremost, only partly conscious, but it means, unusually I think, the auditor is required to become an actor-within-the-mind. The particular verse, melody and harmony is then filtered through that meditative mask – to what? – to the still observer beyond. As each phase of the cycle concludes, the listener, in the silence between sections, is brought to join, more consciously, his own, still, observation point beyond words, music, character, mask and in this manner transformation appropriate to each person's own standing is effected. The whole experience is a controlled, ritualised journey of such rare beauty, that we are brought to a different place in ourselves. Contained in the *temenos* of performance the participants can experience transformation to new dimensions of being.

In the transformational process, the therapeutic possibilities of performance begin to be noticed. Ancient teaching had music and medicine as two flowers on a single stem, and likewise music and theology were similarly twinned. The gods of music, medicine and theology are brought together in the figure of Hermes, the messenger of the gods – Apollo, Asclepius, Zeus. In the archetypal figure of Orpheus the same range of skills has been noticed: the performer, the priest, the healer, as well as the lover. Small wonder, then, that at this stage of our enquiry we should observe a personal transformation in right-directed performance which contains a therapeutic aspect. The work for the performer is to merge his individual portrait of Orpheus with the archetypal, for the listener then can reach, through more directed meditation, the deep, silent observer – the soul.

CHAPTER SEVEN

With 'wit' and 'will'

O ignorant poor man, what dost thou bear
Lockt up within the casket of thy breast?
What jewels and what riches hast thou there!
What heavenly treasure in so weak a chest!

Look in thy soul, and thou shalt beauties find
Like those which drown'd Narcissus in the flood:
Honour and Pleasure both are in thy mind,
And all that in the world is counted good.[1]

So Sir John Davies begins to wind up his major epic poem on the nature of Man – the English equivalent of the famous oration by Pico della Mirandola of the neo-Platonic school of Ficino, one hundred years before, *On the Dignity of Man*. Davies' poem, called *Nosce teipsum: of Human Knowledge*, spins out over 482 four-line rhyming stanzas, in a superb monument to the searching mind of the Elizabethan Age to find order and understanding in all things. It is a summation of all that was understood of human psychology at the time, with reference to the soul. It deserves to be far better known than it is, and repays close study from several points of view: the subject matter; the manner of telling; and the organisation of the material. This chapter presents some of his argument, partly in diagram form, then goes on to consider several general points in relation to the soul and performance. Finally, in a diagram echoing the first on the human frame, the inspirational line of expression of the 'soul of performance' is attempted. Through all this the 'maid-servants to the soul', 'wit' and 'will', will be in service.

Here is a diagram which presents a Renaissance view of Man, in its barest essentials:

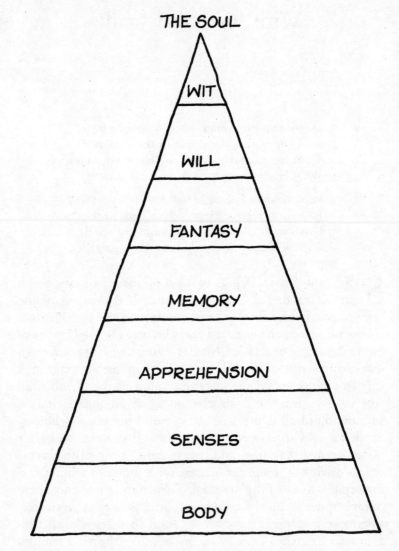

THE SOUL

WIT

WILL

FANTASY

MEMORY

APPREHENSION

SENSES

BODY

Figure 13

This generalised view would serve as a general picture, acknowledged as standard, throughout two and a half centuries, from the late fifteenth century onwards. We will consider its parts in detail, calling on Sir John Davies' words to elaborate it.

Davies tells us 'the body is the soul's household', meaning 'body' as the whole diagram, not only the lowest portion, and that all the parts are mutually dependent. The force of 'spirit' binds all parts together (as was discussed in Chapter 6), which force emanates from out of the soul and returns to it. However, the soul remains completely still, the unmoving observer, a little spark of the Divine creator.

From the soul let us move to the farthest extremity of our being, to the level of 'body', which Sir John Davies describes as 'a dwelling place'. The body is an unthinking, dense prison of matter in which the soul is encased for our brief lifespan. In Shakespeare's words 'a muddy vesture of decay, which doth grossly close it [the soul] in'. But Davies is not only critical of the body as a snare: in keeping with his positive outlook, the body, though weak, is a 'treasure chest' for it holds the soul within it. It also reflects Divine grace by being self-maintaining (that is, when the hand is grazed, the body will heal itself) by means of what Davies calls 'the quickening-power', which to him is proof that even the dense body owes its existence to the all-pervading spirit of God. To keep it in good health, and maintain its vital powers is the duty of the higher parts of our being, for of itself it has no choice, taking only what is decided for it from above. At death the body returns to the basic elements of which it was made, earth, water, air and fire.

The 'senses', five of them, are described as 'the windows' which 'searcheth all things'. They do not have discriminating powers, but are open to 'all things', without exception. They are the means by which the soul communicates with the world of sense, the physical world and by which the world communicates with the soul. They are the soul's 'intelligencers' (Robert Jones' preface p. 15). The five senses form two

distinct levels: smell, taste, and feeling belong to the body and
are the lower senses, providing essential information for good
functioning; sight and hearing feed the mind, which is why
Davies says they are placed high in the head, so as to serve the
mind more directly. The information that the senses bring is
so diverse, so constant (for they never sleep), so frequently
delightful, so full of potential danger, that many men are in
danger of losing contact with their higher self and become
locked in body and sense alone. They are then, Davies considers, less than brute beasts and have negated the fundamental dignity accorded to men by God. For a full life, it is our
duty to cross the threshold into the subtler parts of our being.

The threshold into this miraculous 'inner creation, this
Aladdin's cave of riches', is called 'apprehension', and is
described as 'a porter admitting all'. Apprehension carries, or
transmits, everything the senses deliver, without discrimination. Like a hotel porter, all the baggage delivered by the
endless variety of guests and dumped in the foyer is carried to
the various appropriate rooms. That is apprehension at
work, taking things in. Going out, there is discrimination
at work, for the outward transmitting of apprehension is
ordered by the higher parts. If the inner man is in good order,
then the outward baggage will also be in good shape. The
condition of the material moved from within to without
reflects directly the condition of the inner state. A trained
observer watching the outgoing baggage knows exactly the
inner situation. Ficino says, 'what we see is the shape of his
soul'! But more of this in a moment. Apprehension does not
in itself judge or discriminate, but merely does what is asked
of it, like the faithful servant he is.

Now moving into the grand mansion of the mind, we are
faced with a bewildering array of rooms, each with its own
character. Perhaps 'department store' would make a better
metaphor, for the riches are beyond counting. Here Davies
attempts *not* to be encyclopaedic, but deliberately non-
definitive. Nevertheless, his direct, almost naive, approach
has something to teach our mind-watchers of today. He

begins with 'memory', which later turns out to be in two parts: lower memory, which is 'the storehouse' of information, facts, habits, like the filing-cabinet of the mind. Everything brought in by the porter, from the ceaselessly working senses is stored, without discrimination. The degree of order will vary wildly, not only from person to person, but also from subject to subject, depending on many factors, including how we relate to different areas of endeavour and compartments of knowledge. So 'lower memory' may be very neat and tidy in some sections, whilst being totally in disarray in others. Some of this comes across to the outside world as difference of personality, when in fact it is a reflection of order or disorder higher up the levels of being.

'Higher memory' comes higher up the ladder, surrounding 'fantasy' and at times feeding it, yet it is linked with lower memory, and has some traits in common. We see here one of the shortcomings of a diagrammatic scheme – something multidimensional reduced to only two, yet if we keep in mind its limitations it has a useful function to perform. Imagine, then, 'fantasy' surrounded by 'lower memory' below and 'upper memory' above, and yet those two having links or channels to each other, like tunnels through 'fantasy'. We will consider the nature of 'higher memory' first. These are often ancient memories, and are described as 'deep' and 'silent', as opposed to the surface chatter of lower memory. In modern terminology, this is where 'archetypal' memory is found – where we store myth, legend, symbol, and where 'racial memory' might be stored (though Davies does not raise this!). It is an area, of its nature, strange and unknown yet of fundamental importance. It is an area of mystery, and therefore for the developing individual an area where much work must be done. I would guess though that Davies would caution an excess of attention to this area at the expense of the higher parts, for 'higher memory' still cannot act of its own volition.

And so to 'fantasy', the exciting part we have all been waiting for. The part of us that compares, dreams, desires, imagines and so must include the more modern term 'imagination'; the area that deals with 'images' in a creative way. We often speak of 'idle fantasy', or 'riotous imagination' or 'creative genius' or 'destructive fantasy', suggesting very clearly that 'fantasy' is neither good nor bad of its own essence, but depends on other things for its health and well-being. For our stated interest in this present book, the world of the performer, it is a region of prime importance to understand. Davies tells us that 'fantasy' is the 'handmaid to the mind'. This tells us three interesting things: first, he regards 'fantasy' as feminine; second, he does not believe we have yet reached a region he would call 'mind', yet we would place 'fantasy' firmly there; third, it suggests that fantasy is yet another servant to a higher authority.

In the feminine fantasy of Sir John Davies' scheme we see 'a busy power working day and night' who 'sits and beholds, and doth discern the all,/Compounds in one thing divers of their kind;/Compares the black and white, the great and small'. She muses and takes inspiration from all that the body, the senses and apprehension and memory lay before her, and from these, 'fantastical sprites' may spring. There would seem to be no limit to the play of the imagination in our own direct experience, yet Davies is all the time suggesting it must be ordered from above, for the creative imagination to have fruitful manifestation. Here is a lesson for the artist, the performer, and those with a creative bent.

Ascending this stairway of Man, we come to the highest regions of 'will' and 'wit' – placed diagrammatically wit above will, though in reality the two occupy a position alongside each other. Philosophers have debated for thousands of years the relative position of heart and mind, for these are the nearest, yet not quite, equivalents to 'will' and 'wit'. Both are described by Davies as 'maidservants to the soul', the equivalent of the soul's right and left hands.

'Will' is that 'through which the soul tunes the body' and is the seat of Love. 'Will' contains the passions, hope, joy, hate, fear, grief and the rest of all human emotions. It is the organ of action, of choosing and, in its purest state seeks and desires only 'the Good'.

'Wit' is 'the pupil of the soul's clear eye' and is the seat of knowledge. Here the soul exercises reason, discrimination, understanding, enjoys contemplation, and is able to judge. The ultimate activity of 'wit' is in seeking 'the Truth'.

It will be clear from Davies' definition of 'wit' and 'will' that he sees these two areas of the human frame as of profound importance. Through them the soul, itself unmoving, acts and directs the rest of the body, including the potentially unruly 'fantasy'. The 'love' of 'will' is no ordinary love, but love of the Divine, as perceived through the soul, a fragment of the Divine. Nor is the 'knowledge' of 'wit' anything like bookish knowledge or anything that can be learned in school. This is nothing less than a desire for knowledge of the Divine, again as perceived through the soul.

Imagine creative action, in the arts, undertaken with the whole being tuned in Davies' system. With a clarity and directness, like mountain air or a ray of the sun, the soul would pass inspiration direct from apprehension of the Divine through the discriminative powers, and fired through the untainted passions into the melting-pot of 'fantasy', there to be poured into a myriad of undreamed forms out into the lower world in the shape of poetry, music, painting, sculpture, dance, theatre and the rest carrying an undiffused vision of 'divine frenzy'! This then, in Sir John Davies' mind is the reason for the need for *nosce teipsum* – 'know thyself'. From Plato through the Ficino academy at Careggi to the Elizabethan poet-philosopher, this dictum still resonates with a pristine power. 'God', says Davies, 'is Alpha to wit and Omega to will'. The whole created universe is embraced in their compass. The soul continually fashions itself and completes itself by the unending exercise of wit and will.

As we well know, however, the soul's sojourn in this body is beset with vicissitudes – cunning traps for the unwary set, according to the Christian ethic, by the fall of the first man, Adam. Hermetic and Platonic philosophies have their equivalent stories of how the soul comes to be locked in this small prison. Whilst here, in a Davies' couplet we are advised:

> Soul is tempted whilst on this earth
> By Wisdom, Wealth, Pleasure, Praise.

But there are certain conditions, according to Ficino, which free the soul from everyday concerns and pressures, and open it to higher influence, and thus, when the mind is unoccupied, the soul is refreshed by food of its own nature. These seven conditions are ranged thus:[2]

(1) sleep
(2) syncope (or fainting)
(3) melancholy
(4) aloneness
(5) reverie
(6) chastity of mind
(7) devotion to God

So perhaps the soul's temptations of wisdom, wealth, pleasure and praise, (a constant stream of each for the successful performer!), are to some degree tempered by the seven states where the soul is said to gain relief from these pressures. It is comforting to know that in sleep the soul is thus refreshed, and the matter is literally taken out of our hands. Some of these other states, familiar to Ficino no doubt, need some exploring, for me at least, before a fuller understanding of their nature can grow.

We can take heart, in the midst of this high-flown, near-mystical dialogue with the soul, that again and again the neo-Platonic writers return to the efficacy of performance as a means of uniting soul and body to a higher understanding. In performance, rightly directed, transformation really does take place. Performance can create devices 'to devise variety of endless pleasure to delight the senses', and may end there. Yet that, too, can be just a first step. The arts must delight in order to attract our further attention, and lead us subtly to a more profound contemplation. This happens in seven stages during a performance as it:

(a) delights the senses
(b) invites curiosity
(c) involves the mind
(d) encourages deeper study
(e) encourages regular practice
(f) expands love
(g) opens up knowledge

No stage can be omitted; all are dependent on each other.

Performance belongs closely to the essential dignity of man, as outlined by Pico della Mirandola through to Sir John Davies, for of all God's creation only man has the power to create. In creating the arts we imitate what God does – we create in order to enjoy our creation. The human mind can conceive of possibilities that are not yet manifest (that is, we can uncover the possibilities of existence in the mind of God). Man prolongs the divine act of creation and man fashions himself through art, for the soul provides an image of itself expressed externally, as a mirror images the viewer. In other words, man (as God) creates; what is created is him (as God's creation).

There are three stages of initiation on this transformation journey which are described by Ficino, and then elaborated by one of his French philosopher followers, Pontus de Tiehard:[3]

 (i) the union of poetry and music
 (ii) the study of ideas
(iii) the study of things divine

Ficino also discusses the first stage as arising naturally from conversation with equals which leads in good company to the enjoyment of songs and instrumental music. 'In this way', he says, 'the creative soul is brought into the light.'

Art is an endeavour to impose order on formlessness and hence is an expression of Love (echoing the descent of Eros to form order out of chaos amongst the warring elements). Love is the power which produces all things – procreation, no less. Orphic fragments describe Love as having a threefold nature:

(a)   he is inventive and playful
(b)   he is double-natured and changeable
(c)   he holds the key to everything

This makes him a tricky customer to deal with, yet, since he holds the key to everything, there is no other way – all harmonious interplay is Love manifesting.

We have seen the fourfold nature of Orpheus before but with Love playing through his masks, he can appear like this:

(i)   the civiliser – love for his fellows
(ii)   the thelogian – love as a cosmic force
(iii)   the artist – imposing order
(iv)   the lover – enjoying a vision of divine bliss

Through Orpheus, through the arts, God puts down a helping hand to lift us up.

The consideration of this image, immortalised in the painting by Nicholas Hilliard, brings to mind a second hierarchy of seven levels as a further aid to the performer. The information for this is not so neatly embodied in a poem, or a philosophical tract, but is scattered through diverse prefaces in the English lute song repertoire. Two we have already seen – Dowland's *First Booke* and Jones' *Third Booke*. These are models of their kind, from among more than thirty such prefaces existing, all containing a part of a larger body of knowledge in relation to the position of the performer, to those above and below him.[4] For us, as performers, to be more able servants is to know our place as well.

Some of these labels seem a trifle strange at first so let us consider each degree. God (or Apollo), self-explanatory,

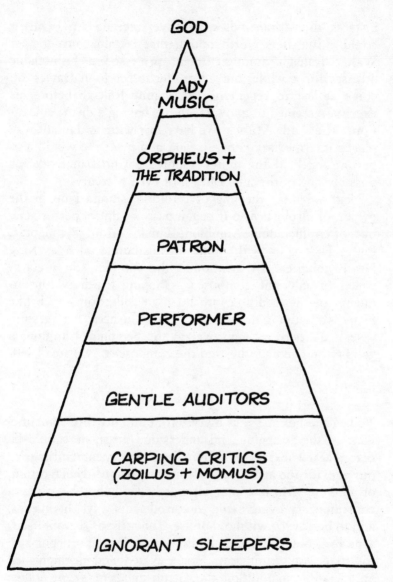

Figure 14

inspires all, without whose creative force no arts or artist could exist. (It is worth noting that certain courtiers, Sir Walter Raleigh amongst them, professed a fashionable atheism for a while, but according to Sir John Davies 'all come at last to repentance'. Certainly Raleigh before his execution seemed to allow for things having a divine emanation.) The 'Lady Musick' we have met with as the half-way placed intermediary between God and men; she would also be an 'angel', if the writer adopted a Christian mode, or possibly one of the nine Muses, or even Mercury.

Next we meet the line of tradition, summed up in the person of Orpheus as our pagan patron saint of performers, but often including Amphion, Linus, Arion, Pythagoras, Plato, Ficino, or with biblical contributors such as King David, Jubal etc. By mentioning this tradition, the preface-writer (usually the composer) is hoping to 'draw' the influence of the tradition into his own collection (much like Ficino's attempt to draw down astral influences). This gesture reveals a desire for approval in the perennial tradition, a validity and veracity beyond the composer's own small self.

THE ARTIST AS SERVANT

Today, the next stage is awry. From an outworn 'romantic' view of the struggling, misunderstood artist, he should be placed at the next level. Therein lies a fundamental mistake of our age, for the artist is a servant, not only of the Tradition, or of Lady Musick, and ultimately God, but he needs a contemporary living being to consider his ways, his means, and to bestow or withhold praise. The artist as servant *needs* a patron, not only for essential economic support, but also for precise discrimination, for elevated and distinguished appreciation. In addition, the patron *stands in for the Divine* as an earthly representative. This is the fullest potential of the patron, hence the terms of exaggerated praise to be found in many of these dedications – the artist is consciously addressing the Divine in his understanding patron, in the full expectation that the Divine will respond, with largesse of many kinds. Cash is only one of numerous kinds of reward. Some time soon I feel I must write a book on this very stage in the hierarchy, for until our own time has a better grasp of this position, the arts will remain dis-eased and weak. It is difficult to address the Divine in our present fashion for *sponsorship*, the nearest, debased equivalent of patronage. We must study patronage in history and across a worldwide geography, and digest this data in order to begin to comprehend the appropriate manifestation of patronage for the new time to come.

The next level, of performer, has been the subject of this book, so perhaps sufficient has been said about this level. Though the performer is a servant to the higher authorities, this is of course in no way demeaning. The self-respect and optimism of the performer is essential to his role-play. His humility is a necessary balance to his self-assuredness. This balance comes through in a number of the lute songbook prefaces.

Likewise the position of the 'gentle auditor' has been stated several times during the course of this exposition. The addition of 'gentle' ennobles the position of the listener, and encourages an active response to the performance. Much has been made of audience participation in recent years, but rarely has it been pointed out that while externally still, an audience may be inwardly contributing as much as the performer. I hope this book has shown how vital this participation is, for it was certainly clear to the commentators 400 years ago.

Now to the curious section of carping critics (Zoilus and Momus). It is surprising how many dedications and prefaces raise the names of these two notorious critics of the ancient world. Homer was long dead and could not reply to honour his own name, yet Zoilus, a third-rate grammarian threw the rule book at him, and proceeded to demolish all that was good in Homer. At least, that is what he set out to do. In Monteverdi's day, Artusi began a prolonged attack on his disregard for the rules. At the same time one Gabriel Harvey, in England, lambasted the works of poets finer than himself. Today we have music critics like Richard Dyer in Boston, or Tom Sutcliffe in London, who perpetrate acidic criticism of the most bilious, ulcerous kind, with the artists so attacked having no channel or right of reply. Momus Sutcliffe and Zoilus Dyer should know that the Renaissance hierarchy had a place for them, beneath the dignity of the artist, or their gentle auditors.

In fact, below the distorted views of dyspeptic critics, only one level remains – that of the ignorant sleepers, who would rarely wake to stir to the sounds of divine inspiration. These men of clay or lead, are, however, as essential to the stability of the hierarchy as every other level. And that is the good, creative news – everyone has a part to play whether they know it or not – consciousness rises at every step.

CHAPTER EIGHT

An outline for a future course of music study

THERE is a simple equation which relates to inspiration and performance: the more thoroughly prepared the performer is in all aspects of *decoro*, and the more boldly the performer embraces *sprezzatura* in the moment of performance the greater are the possibilities of revealing the Orpheus within. When Orpheus steps forward singing new songs of divine inspiration, then Euridice is enticed from out of the audience and the oldest reactions of the myth are re-enacted – Orpheus and Euridice are united in love and harmony.

But 'preparation', as for any ritual of significance, is vital. To prepare this generation in the enlivened performing arts we require a new statement of *musica speculativa* which will serve into the next millennium. It must be emphasised that *musica speculativa* is not a fancy name for music theory as taught in our colleges and universities, or as outlined in the grade exams of the Associated Board. That music theory is the intellectual rationalising of centuries of music practice and compositional procedures and is important in its place. However *musica speculativa* is of a different order altogether, for it is concerned with the world of concepts, with the philosophy of music. It was, in the Mediaeval and Renaissance tradition, the bridge between *musica instrumentalis* (the making of human music) on the one hand, and the *musica mundana* or world music (the music of the spheres) on the other. Only in part does *speculativa* coincide with the concerns of intellectual music theory, its importance lies elsewhere.

The greatest task immediately ahead of us in my opinion is to restate the essence of *musica speculativa* for our time, to state afresh a philosophy of the performing arts so that once again they may serve the highest aspirations of humanity. This book must conclude with a brief survey of this subject, for its purpose has been to bring the reader to this threshold. However, the task of establishing a new *musica speculativa* will not be achieved in one brief chapter, nor in one book, nor by one writer, but will be developed corporately over a decade or so of very carefully directed activity, observations and exchange. The material in this book provides a focus or basis for practical work with groups of students working on the art of performance. The rest of this chapter provides the conceptual basis for directing that study. The very study will refine what is contained here, and will out-mode it. The results of the practical work over the next decade will provide the material for the next book.

The conceptual framework is drawn from working with the 'ancient theology' or 'perennial philosophy' and thus draws on ancient wisdom without being bound by specific creeds. At the heart, it needs to be acknowledged that the created universe is an instrument of Divine will, whose music cannot be known by us directly. By the use of contemplation and the power of inspiration, certain features of this divine music might be revealed. By the use of metaphor and similitudes something of this conceptual realm can be communicated. The ineffable mystery of the power of performance is more fully appreciated and the serious student advances by small degrees. The central mystery remains, but the individual relationship to it is enhanced.

Here is a plan to bring this appreciation of music into focus: the essential materials to consider are five in number, namely, the music; the instrument; the performer; the listener; the space. It is perhaps not necessary to remind you that it is not the mundane manifestation of these five aspects that we are studying, but their subtle or conceptual states.

Our perception might expand in the following manner, as we study each of these in turn.

1 *The Music*: Conceptual music has three main facets, pulse, melody and harmony. Pulse, discussed mundanely as rhythm, is the first manifestation of creation, the first vibration emanating from the creator. Pulse holds all creation in place, including music and all other human activities. There are a number of simple exercises to practise in small groups which reveal the power of pulse, its organisational abilities, and its utter dependability. Pulse moves from rest, to action, to rest unendingly – the performer who has become truly familiar with that law is working from a reliable foundation. To grasp it intellectually is so easy it seems like child's play, but to know it in practice is to understand it *is* child's play.

Following naturally from the contemplation of pulse (and the play of numbers that flows with it) comes melody, but this is no ordinary tune or jingle. In deep contemplation, the knowledge of pulse as the underlying principle of creation causes a response, a certain lifting and stirring of the spirit. Various pitches or intervals express the soul in flight, now high, now low and the very movement makes melody. A thanksgiving song is uttered for the existence of creation itself – pulse. The nearest man-made music comes to expressing this conceptual level of melody is in the slow soul-searching *alap* of a classical Indian master such as Ram Naryan. He coaxes, with such gentle sensuality, a primeval use of finely-tuned intervals – creation's morning song of thanksgiving.

Bearing witness to the birth of melody is the steady gaze of God, watching his creation unfolding in song, held in place gently but securely by his own emanation, pulse. The two dance together, pulse and melody, and together express love, which is harmony. So full of joy is harmony that its varieties of expression can never be exhausted. Take the harmonic resonances of chanting Tibetan monks, or the ululating of Bulgarian peasant girls. Contrast the choiring angels of six-part polyphony of Josquin, or the astonishing dissonances of a Gesualdo madrigal, the acerbic interplay of instruments in Stravinsky's *The Rite of Spring*, or the harmonic loftiness of Bach's *Art of Fugue*. Harmony is intoxication, it is God in love with his own creation.

In the new *musica speculativa*, when the word 'music' is used, it refers then to the conceptual level of pulse, melody and harmony in this inspirational sense. I would expect that the first introduction in a practical course to these concepts might take up the major part of a term, though a life-time of returning for inspiration is not unlikely. A second term might proceed in the following manner.

2   *The Instrument*: It is necessary to address ourselves to the means by which the pulse, melody and harmony are manifested. How does this love-song resound, but through all of creation? The five elements: earth, water, fire, air and ether carry the resonance to every part of creation. Even in this atomic age, the ancient elements serve well to discuss the nature of this grand instrument. It is in metaphor that these ideas are best expressed and best understood. The heavy Earth contains the seed. All future creative possibilities are held, safe in Earth until the right moment for expression. The material aspects of all instruments, be it the human voice, the Koto, the symphony orchestra or the electronic organ, are held in Earth. What is the conceptual nature of subtle Earth? How does it transform from a heavy clay to a light friable loam? And what are the Earth aspects with which the inspired performer needs to keep in touch? Can the singer express the Earth element of his or her voice and use it as a foundation for technique?

Next, water, which subtly binds creation together. A performance which does not flow, no matter how technically perfect, will not move us. The Water element binds and bonds in love, and can suffuse every part of the heavier Earth. What give and take, what ebbing and flowing is required in Mozart's string quartets, for example? The elevated dialogue of great chamber music plays through the Water element and carries the willing listener to an ocean of experience. The fluidity with which one of the great Indian singers like Parween Sultana transverses the lowest to highest notes of her extraordinary range is like swimming in the depths of the most beautiful azured water. The momentum from one note to the next, in all music, is the simple powerful current of subtle Water.

Traditionally craftmanship is associated with the element Fire, for in Fire the form of things is made manifest. To survey the musical instruments of the world, of past as well as present, is to witness the inspirations of countless nameless craftsmen. Amongst the most beautiful works of art of all times are musical instruments made to resound in the hands of Orpheus: the great organ which occupies the gallery of five floors of a department store in Philadelphia; the violins not only of the justly famed Stradivarius or Amanti, but of the numerous incredibly fine anonymous luthiers of the seventeenth century. Or the fragments of instruments that survive from the ancient world – harps from Babylon and Egypt that inspire still for their beauty if no longer for their sound. Again the simple crudity of aboriginal instruments, where the maker and player are often one and the same. The rasping wail of a one-stringed rebab joined with the fiery voice of a toothless Orpheus is timeless in its effect. But mere human craftsmanship, so varied and inspiring as it is in our world of musical instruments, is a pale shadow of the fire of inspiration of the Divine craftsman in fashioning the world instrument. A lifelong contemplation of this wonder will reveal but a tiny part of the intricacy and skill of His craftsmanship. The lightest lute, strung to bursting point, acts as an inspirational symbol of the fiery nature of form and craftsmanship, but it is but a shadow compared to the universal lute.

Many instruments share the feature of enclosing a volume of air, but subtle Air interpenetrates more solid materials – an observation made by the ancients now seemingly corroborated by recent findings by nuclear physicists. The sense of touch has been traditionally associated with the element Air, and 'Dowland, whose touch upon the lute doth ravish human sense' reminds us that for the musician this element and this sense need great refinement of awareness. Air and breath obviously work closely together, and the matter of breathing is essential to the musician. Not only the singer relies on developed breath control, for any music must 'breathe' to move organically, rhythmically and comfortably. Indeed the need for breath links us directly, and vitally, to pulse. Musicians, and artists generally, are often said to 'have their heads in the clouds', but this might be more accurate than is generally realised. There, in a rarefied air on the upper slopes of Mount Parnassus, inspiration comes through strong and clean. The air is good there, and not a little intoxicating.

Here in this world of form these four elements of Earth, Water, Fire and Air inform if studied in this refreshing way. Eventually awareness wakes to a fifth element, the 'quintessence', Ether, said in traditional teaching to be the most subtle of the five and interpenetrating the four denser elements. In Vedic teaching it is the lifegiving *prana*, yet modern science has still to identify and confirm its existence. Nevertheless, tradition states that Ether carries unmanifest sound, yet links with the sense of hearing. If you consider that four elements make up the physical universe, and that there is a similar four-part division in the unmanifest creation, Ether is the connecting point between the two.

By this means subtle vibration (or pulse) is brought from the unmanifest creation via ether to the world of sense. Perhaps the ancient stories of music making stones to be built, or collapse, and trees to dance may arise from this etheric transmission. It is not necessary, however, to entertain such obscure stories to understand the relationship of ether and sound, for in performance the performer is aware of a palpable quality penetrating the air, carrying sound to the listener. Since this element is supraphysical, it is not surprising that physical science has not been able to isolate it and examine the substance 'ether'.

This brief sketch of the five parts of the Instrument

An outline for a future course of music study

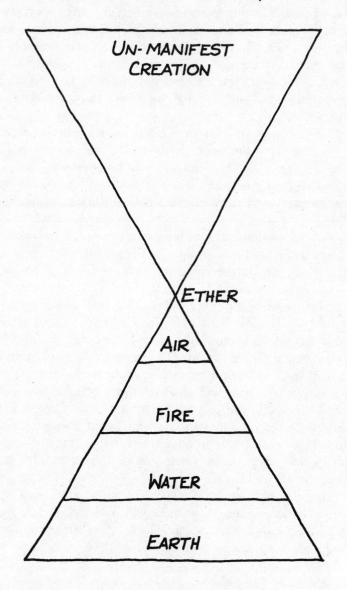

Figure 15

introduces a way of contemplating nature which has immense practical value to the performer. A study programme might proceed, over a term, to take each element in turn and work for a week in depth isolating the separate elements in performance, discussion and meditation. The second half of term will then synthesise all five in practice. I have no doubt the experience of such a programme will be of breathtaking dimensions.

3   *The Performer*: Since the entire book has been devoted to this aspect little more needs to be said at this point. However, most of the attention has been dwelling on the individual performer, and it is easy to forget the conceptual level: namely, what does the small performer symbolise? Behind every performer there is an impelling force which lies beyond the individual, and that is *the force of creative expression*. It is, in its origins, a Divine force which needs must manifest. On the route through the levels of creation much energy is absorbed, but this allows us to enjoy the play of creative expression without being blinded, as we certainly would be by the first burst of creative activity. Mozart at five, and frequently throughout his short life, expressed this force in relatively undiluted form. The strength of the tradition of study in Indian classical music allows the performer to learn to transmit a very direct creative force. After all the individual is not allowed to perform for very many years, until the guru perceives the artist has developed a vessel strong enough to cope with undiluted creative energy. We are playing with fire in this work – indeed right training is a matter of life and death.

From the performer's inner being come three essential desires, and the strength of these will probably dictate how well the performer succeeds in his work. In their purest form these desires are simple and may be expressed as:

> a desire to sing the song
> a desire for aspiration
> a desire for unity

but of course every individual performer will develop a unique way of describing why they think they want to perform. It is good, though, to come to a conceptual clarity at times, so that the daily effort is re-inspired by these considerations. When the performer remembers that it is essentially the desire to sing *the* song that got him into this difficult or tedious recording session, energy is renewed.

4   *The Listener*: During the course of this book quite a bit has inevitably been said about the listener, but a few words more will show how the performer and listener provide, conceptually speaking, a perfect coupling – male and female counterparts, symbolised in Orpheus and Euridice. Their mating or union is the just outcome of inspired performance.

If the performer is the giver, the point of activity, so the listener is the receiver. As the performer channels the force of creative expression, so the listener experiences the *pull* of creative expression and is drawn out of a Stygian-like dark abode into the light by the power of Orpheus' song, hands outstretched, coming into fuller life and light.

The three desires, expressed in the performer, find their equivalent in the listener as three longings:

    a longing for peace
    a longing for uplift
    a longing for unity

In every breast is a degree of turbulence, creating a longing for peace, closely followed by a longing to be raised to a higher state of awareness. Out of this is revealed, deepest of all, a longing to be reunited. With Orpheus' song, channelling divine frenzy, Euridice's longings are assuaged.

5   *The Space*: A respectful study of the space in which performance takes place completes this brief survey of a new *musica speculativa* for our time. The concept of *temenos* has already been discussed, but much practical work, in study groups on performance and space, needs to be undertaken in order that an ancient idea can take on new life. Logically, and on the most basic level, performance and audience must

occupy a space. The quality of the experience will to some degree be dictated by the quality of the space. Much more care needs to be taken on the preparation of the performing space to be sure that the concept *temenos* can work to its fullest. A familiarity with some of the great performing places of the past will enrich our understanding of the unique contribution 'space' can make to performance. I think particularly of the sequence of rooms in the Castello of Ferrara which move from large, open spaces down to the casket-like jewel of a room in which Duke Alfonso's *musica secreta* was performed by the famed *concerto delle donne*. The room, stage or arena creates an all-enfolding quality, womblike and protective, nursing a delicate creation into being. The right music in the right space at the right time creates a buoyancy which uplifts and inspires. The very walls respond to the vibration of sound, and somehow contribute to the quality of vibration.

Like some extraordinary piece of alchemical equipment, the alembic of performance nurses an experiment which leaves behind a residue of subtle gold. This Orphic gold is proof that our experiment has come to fullness and fruition. But a fuller understanding of this mystery will be ours as we engage in the work that still lies ahead.

Ime ftands ftill

Lute-songs on the theme of
mutability and metamorphosis
by John Dowland and his contemporaries.

An Englishman in the Renaissance had an abiding interest in
and fascination for mutability or change. Edmund Spenser's
great unfinished epic of renaissance courtly love abruptly
ends with the 'Mutabilitie Cantos', songs of change, which
opens with these lines:

> What man that sees ever-whirling wheels
> Of Change, the which all mortal things doth sway,
> But that thereby doth find and plainly feele
> How Mutability in them doth play
> Her cruell sports, to many men's decay?

The notion was that all beneath the Moon – the world, the
four elements, man, all creatures and plants were subject to
change or decay. Above the Moon, in the heavenly spheres,
Time had no power.

Such ideas of metamorphosis were a source of perennial

inspiration to poets, particularly those writing lyric poetry. Hence many of the texts for the lute-song repertoire dwell on the themes arising from this passion. The twelve songs of this programme present twelve uses of the theme of change, some light and humorous, others more weighty and contemplative. We conclude with the concept that through art, rightly proportioned, Man's experience may be that 'Time Stands Still'.

'TIME STANDS STILL'

1. His Goulden Locks time hath to silver turnde – John Dowland
2. Though you are young and I am old   – Thomas Campion
3. Come chearfull day   – Thomas Campion
4. It was a time when silly bees could speak – John Dowland
5. Go passions to the cruell fayre   – Thomas Ford
6. Farre from Triumphing Courte   – John Dowland
7. Now each creature   – George Handford
8. Time, cruell Time   – John Danyel
9. He whose desires   – John Danyel
10. Flow not so fast ye fountains   – John Dowland
11. What then is love but mourning   – Philip Rosseter
12. Time Stands Still with gazing on her face – John Dowland

1

His golden locks Time hath to silver turned.
　　O Time too swift! O swiftness never ceasing!
His youth 'gainst Time and Age hath ever spurned,
　　But spurned in vain; youth waneth by increasing.
Beauty, strength, youth are flowers but fading seen;
Duty, faith, love are roots and ever green.

His helmet now shall make a hive for bees,
　　And lover's sonnets turn to holy psalms.
A man-at-arms must now serve on his knees,
　　And feed on prayers which are Age's alms.
But though from Court to cottage he depart,
His Saint is sure of his unspotted heart.

And when he saddest sits in homely cell,
  He'll teach his swains this carol for a song:
Blest be the hearts that wish my Sovereign well.
  Curst be the soul that think her any wrong.
Goddess, allow this aged man his right
To be your bedesman now that was your knight.
                                  ?Sir Henry Lee

2

THOUGH you are young and I am old,
Though your veins hot and my blood cold,
Though youth is moist and age is dry,
Yet embers live when flames do die.

The tender graft is eas'ly broke,
But who shall shake the sturdy oak?
You are more fresh and fair than I,
Yet stubs do live when flowers do die.

Thou, that thy youth dost vainly boast,
Know, buds are soonest nipped with frost.
Think that thy fortune still doth cry:
Thou fool, to-morrow thou must die.

3

COME, cheerful day, part of my life, to me;
  For while thou view'st me with thy fading light,
Part of my life doth still depart with thee,
  And I still onward haste to my last night.
Time's fatal wings do ever forward fly,
So every day we live a day we die.

But, O ye nights, ordained for barren rest,
  How are my days deprived of life in you;
When heavy sleep my soul hath dispossessed
  By feigned death life sweetly to renew.
Part of my life in that you life deny;
So every day we live a day we die.

4

IT was a time when silly bees could speak,
  And in that time I was a silly bee,
Who fed on time until my heart 'gan break,
  Yet never found the time would favour me.
Of all the swarm I only did not thrive,
Yet brought I wax and honey to the hive.

Then thus I buzzed when time no sap would give:
  Why should this blessed time to me be dry,
Sith by this time the lazy drone doth live,
  The wasp, the worm, the gnat, the butterfly.
Mated with grief I kneeled on my knees,
And thus complained unto the king of bees:

My liege, gods grant thy time may never end,
  And yet vouchsafe to hear my plaint of time,
Which fruitless flies have found to have a friend,
  And I cast down when atomies do climb.
The king replied but thus: Peace, peevish bee,
Thou'rt bound to serve the time, the time not thee.
                    Ascribed to Robert, Earl of Essex

5

GO, Passions, to the cruell fair,
  Plead my sorrows never ceasing;
Tell her those smiles are empty air,
  Growing hopes but not increasing,
Hasting, wasting, with swift pace,
Date of joy in dull disgrace.

Urge her, but gently, I request,
  With breach of faith and wrack of vows;
Say that my grief and mind's unrest
  Lives in the shadow of her brows,
Plying, flying, there to die
In sad woe and misery.

Importune pity at the last,
  (Pity in those eyes should hover);
Recount my sighs and torments past

As annals of a constant lover
Spending, ending, many days
Of blasted hopes and slack delays.

6

FAR from triumphing Court and wonted glory
    He dwelt in shady unfrequented places,
Time's prisoner now, he made his pastime story;
    Gladly forgets Court's erst-afforded graces.
That goddess whom he served to heaven is gone,
And he on earth in darkness left to moan.

But lo, a glorious light from his dark rest
    Shone from the place where erst this goddess dwelt;
A light whose beams the world with fruit hath blest;
    Blest was the knight while he that light beheld.
Since then a star fixed on his head hath shined,
And a saint's image in his heart is shrined.

Ravished with joy, so graced by such a saint,
    He quite forgat his cell and self denaid;
He thought it shame in thankfulness to faint,
    Debts due to princes must be duly paid;
Nothing so hateful to a noble mind
As finding kindness for to prove unkind.

But ah! poor knight, though thus in dream he ranged,
    Hoping to serve this saint in sort most meet,
Time with his golden locks to silver changed
    Hath with age-fetters bound him hands and feet.
Ay me! he cries, goddess, my limbs grow faint,
Though I Time's prisoner be, be you my saint.
                                        Sir Henry Lee

7

NOW each creature joys the other,
    Passing happy days and hours;
One bird reports unto another
    In the fall of silver showers;
Whilst the earth, our common mother,
    Hath her bosom decked with flowers.

Whilst the greatest torch of heaven
   With bright rays, warms Flora's lap,
Now making nights and days both even,
   Cheering the plants with fresher sap,
My field of flowers, quite bereaven,
   Wants refresh of better hap.

Echo, daughter of the air,
   Babbling guest of rocks and hills,
Doth know the name of my fierce fair,
   And sounds the accents of my ills.
Each thing pities my despair,
   Whilst that she her lover kills.

Whilst that she, O cruel maid,
   Doth me and my love despise,
My life's flourish is decayed,
   The which depended on her eyes.
But her will must be obeyed,
   And well he ends for love who dies.
                    Samuel Daniel

8

TIME, cruel Time, canst thou subdue that brow
   That conquers all but thee, and thee too stays,
As if she were exempt from scythe or bow,
   From love and years, unsubject to decays?
Or art thou grown in league with those fair eyes,
   That they might help thee to consume our days?
Or dost thou love her for her cruelties,
   Being merciless like thee that no man weighs?
Then do so still, although she makes no 'steem
   Of days nor years, but lets them run in vain.
Hold still thy swift-winged hours, that wond'ring seem
   To gaze on her, even to turn back again;
And do so still, although she nothing cares.
   Do as I do, love her although unkind.
Hold still. Yet, O I fear, at unawares
   Thou wilt beguile her though thou seem'st so kind.
                    Samuel Daniel

9

HE, whose desires are still abroad, I see
   Hath never any peace at home the while;
And therefore now come back my heart to me.
   It is but for superfluous things we toil,
Rest alone with thyself, be all within;
For what without thou gett'st, thou dost not win.
Honour, wealth, glory, fame are no such things
But that which from imagination springs.
High-reaching power, that seems to overgrow,
Doth creep but on the earth, lies base and low.

10

FLOW not so fast, ye fountains;
   What needeth all this haste?
Swell not above your mountains,
   Nor spend your time in waste.
Gentle springs, freshly your salt tears
Must still fall dropping from their spheres.

Weep they space whom Reason
   Or ling'ring Time can ease,
My sorrow can no Season,
   Nor aught besides, appease.
Gentle springs, freshly your salt tears
Must still fall dropping from their spheres.

Time can abate the terror
   Of every common pain;
But common grief is error,
   True grief will still remain.
Gentle springs, freshly your salt tears
Must still fall dropping from their spheres.

11

WHAT then is love but mourning?
What desire but a self-burning?
Till she that hates doth love return,

Thus will I mourn, thus will I sing;
Come away, come away, my darling.

Beauty is but a blooming,
Youth in his glory entombing.
Time hath a while which none can stay.
Then come away while thus I sing:
Come away, come away, my darling.

Summer in winter fadeth;
Gloomy night heavenly light shadeth;
Like to the morn are Venus' flowers,
Such are her hours. Then will I sing:
Come away, come away, my darling.

12

TIME stands still with gazing on her face.
Stand still and gaze, for minutes, hours and years to her give place.
All other things shall change but she remains the same,
Till heavens changed have their course and Time hath lost his
name.
Cupid doth hover up and down, blinded with her fair eyes,
And Fortune captive at her feet contemned and conquered lies.

When Fortune, Love, and Time attend on
Her with my fortunes, love, and time I honour will alone.
If bloodless Envy say Duty hath no desert,
Duty replies that Envy knows herself his faithful heart.
My settled vows and spotless faith no fortune can remove,
Courage shall show my inward faith, and faith shall try my love.

Songs of Mourning:

BEVVAILING
the vntimely death of
Prince *Henry.*

VVorded by THo. CAMPION.

And fet forth to bee fung with one voyce
to the Lute, or Violl :

By *JOHN COPRARIO.*

LONDON:
Printed for *Iohn Browne,* and
are to be fould in S, dunftons
Churchyar , 1 6 1 3.

Songs of Mourning: Bewailing the untimely death of Prince Henry. Worded by Tho. Campion. And set forth to bee sung with one voyce to the Lute, or Violl. 1613

I
To the most sacred King James

O GRIEF, how divers are thy shapes, wherein men languish!
    The face sometime with tears thou fill'st,
        Sometime the heart thou kill'st
          With unseen anguish.
    Sometime thou smil'st to view how Fate
        Plays with our human state.
        So far from surety here
        Are all our earthly joys,
That what our strong hope builds when least we fear,
        A stronger power destroys.

O Fate, why shouldst thou take from kings their joy and
        treasure?
    Their image if men should deface
        'Twere death, which thou dost race
          Even at thy pleasure.
    Wisdom of holy kings yet knows
        Both what it hath and owes.
        Heaven's hostage which you bred
        And nursed with such choice care,
Is ravished now, great King, and from us led
        When we were least aware.

II
To the most sacred Queen Anne

'TIS now dead night, and not a light on earth
        Or star in heaven doth shine.
Let now a mother mourn the noblest birth
        That ever was both mortal and divine.
        O sweetness peerless! More than human grace!
        O flowery beauty! O untimely death!

Now Music fill this place
With thy most doleful breath;
O singing wail a fate more truly funeral
Than when with all his sons the sire of Troy did fall.

Sleep joy, die mirth, and not a smile be seen,
Or show of hearts content;
For never sorrow nearer touched a queen,
Nor were there ever tears more duly spent.
O dear remembrance, full of rueful woe,
O ceaseless passion, O unhuman hour!
No pleasure now can grow,
For withered is her flower.
O anguish! do thy worst and fury tragical,
Since fate in taking one, hath thus disordered all.

III
To the most high and mighty Prince Charles

FORTUNE and glory may be lost and won,
But when the work of Nature is undone
That loss flies past returning.
No help is left but mourning.
What can to kind youth more despiteful prove
Than to be robbed of one sole brother?
Father and mother
Ask reverence, a brother only love.
Like age and birth, like thoughts and pleasures move.
What gain can he heap up, though showers of crowns
descend,
Who for that good must change a brother and a friend?

Follow, O follow yet thy brother's fame;
But not his fate. Let's only change the name,
And find his worth presented
In thee, by him prevented.
Or past example of the dead be great
Out of thyself begin thy story.
Virtue and glory
Are eminent being placed in princely seat.
O heaven, his age prolong with sacred heat,
And on his honoured head let all the blessings light
Which to his brother's life men wished, and wished them right.

IV
To the most princely and virtuous the Lady Elizabeth

So parted you, as if the world for ever
  Had lost with him her light.
  Nor could your tears hard flint to ruth excite.
   Yet may you never
  Your loves again partake in human sight.
O why should Fate such two kind hearts dissever
As Nature never knit more fair or firm together?

  So loved you as sister should a brother,
   Not in a common strain,
  For princely blood doth vulgar fire disdain,
   But you each other
  On earth embraced in a celestial chain.
Alas, for love! that heavenly-born affection
To change should subject be and suffer earth's infection.

V
To the most illustrious and mighty Frederick the fift, Count
Palatine of the Rhine

How like a golden dream you met and parted,
  That pleasing, straight doth vanish.
   O who can ever banish
The thought of one so princely and free-hearted?
But he was pulled up in his prime by Fate,
And love for him must mourn, though all too late.
Tears to the dead are due. Let none forbid
Sad hearts to sigh. True grief cannot be hid.

Yet the most bitter storm to height increased
  By heaven again is ceased.
   O Time, that all things movest,
In grief and joy thou equal measure lovest.
Such the condition is of human life,
Care must with pleasure mix, and peace with strife.
Thoughts with the days must change; as tapers waste,
So must our griefs. Day breaks when night is past.

VI
To *the most disconsolate Great Britain*

WHEN pale Famine fed on thee
   With her unsatiate jaws;
When civil broils set murder free,
   Contemning all thy laws;
When heaven enraged consumed thee so
With plagues that none thy face could know,
Yet in thy looks affliction then showed less
Than now for one's fate all thy parts express.

   Now thy highest states lament
      A son and brother's loss;
   Thy nobles mourn in discontent
      And rue this fatal cross;
Thy Commons are with passion sad
To think how brave a prince they had.
If all thy rocks from white to black should turn,
Yet couldst thou not in show more amply mourn.

VII
To the World

O POOR distracted world, partly a slave
   To pagans' sinful rage, partly obscured
With ignorance of all the means that save,
   And ev'n those parts of thee that live assured
Of heavenly grace, O how they are divided
With doubts late by a kingly pen decided!
   O happy world, if what the sire begun
   Had been closed up by his religious son.

Mourn all you souls oppressed under the yoke
   Of Christian-hating Thrace! Never appeared
More likelihood to have that black league broke,
   For such a heavenly prince might well be feared
Of earthly fiends. O how is zeal inflamed
With power, when Truth wanting defence is shamed.
   O princely soul, rest thou in peace while we
   In thine expect the hopes were ripe in thee.

Notes

CHAPTER ONE

1. Tillyard, E. M. W., *The Elizabethan World Picture*, London, 1943 (reprinted).
2. Dowland, Robert, *A Varietie of Lute Lessons*, London, 1610 (facsimile, London, 1958).
3. e.g. Boyd, M. C., Vale, Marcia, *Elizabethan Music and Music Criticism*, Philadelphia, 1974. *The Gentleman's Recreations*, Cambridge, 1977.
4. Poulton, Diana, *John Dowland*, London, 1972.
5. Salmen, Walter, *Musikgeschichte in Bilden*, Vol. III/9, Leipzig, 1976.
6. Walker, D. P., 'Spiritual and demonic magic; Ficino to Campanella', *Studies of the Warburg Institute*, Vol. 22, London, 1969.
7. Ness, A. J., *The lute music of Francesco da Milano*, Harvard, 1970.
8. Ness, A. J., op. cit.
9. Condivi, Ascaino, *Life of Michelangelo*, Tr. Sir Charles Holroyd, London, 1911.
10. Dowland, Robert, op. cit.
11. Purcell, Henry, *Orpheus Britannicus*, London, 1698 (posthumous collection of songs, facsimile, New York, 1965).
12. Shakespeare, W., *The Merchant of Venice*, (from The Complete Works, Oxford, 1905, reprinted).
13. Castiglione, B., *Il Cortegiano*, Tr. Thomas Hoby, London, 1561 (modern edition Everyman, 1928, reprinted).
14. Peacham, Henry, *The Compleat Gentleman*, London, 1622 (modern edition Oxford, 1906).
15. Self-improvement manuals include: Ascham, R., *The Scholemaster*, London, 1570; Brathwait, R., *The Gentleman's Recreation*, London, 1630; Castiglione, op. cit., Elyot, Sir Thomas, *The boke named the Governour*, London, 1531; Markham, Gervaise, *The Gentleman's Academie*, London, 1595; Peacham, op. cit.

16. Caccini, Giulio, *Le nuove musiche*, Venice, 1602 (modern edition and trans. H. Wiley Hitchcock, Madison, 1982).
17. Caccini, G., op. cit. (preface).
18. Ficino, Marsilio, *Letters*, Vol. II, London, 1975.
19. Ideas presented and explored in: (i) Walker, D. P., op. cit.; (ii) Wallis, R. T., *Neo-platonism*, London, 1972; (iii) Yates, Frances, *The Occult philosophy in the Elizabethan Age*, London, 1979.
20. Dowland, John, *First Booke of Songes*, London, 1597.
21. Jones, Robert, *Ultimum Vale*, London, 1605.

CHAPTER THREE

1. French, P. J., *John Dee*, London, 1972.
2. Dee, John, *Mathematicall Preface*, London, 1570.
3. Butler, Christopher, *Number Symbolism*, London, 1970.

CHAPTER FOUR

1. e.g. Strub, Werner, *Masques pour un théâtre imaginaire*, Paris, 1987; Kennard, J. S., *Masks and Marionettes*, New York, 1935.
2. La Famiglia Carrara, Cooperativa Piccionaia, Vicenza, Italia.
3. Nicoll, Allardyce, *Masks, Mimes and Miracles*, New York, 1931 (reprint, 1963).
4. Fellowes, E. H., *English Madrigal Verse (1588–1632)*, Oxford, 1967.
5. *The English Lute Song Series*, Stainer and Bell Ltd.
6. *English Lute Songs 1597–1632* facsimile reprints (formerly The Scolar Press Ltd, Menston; now Brian Jordan Music and Books, Cambridge).
7. Maynard, John, *XII Wonders of the World*, London, 1611 (modern edition in Stainer and Bell series op. cit.).
8. Tillyard, E. M. W., op. cit.

CHAPTER FIVE

1. Kyd, Thomas, *The Spanish Tragedy*, modern edition in 'The Revels Plays', Manchester, 1985.
2. Dowland, Robert, *A Musicall Banquet*, London, 1610 (No. 10), (facsimile, Menston, 1970).
3. Lyons, B. G., *Voices of Melancholy*, London, 1971.

4. Rooley, Anthony, 'I saw my lady weepe: the first five songs of John Dowland's "Second Book of Songs"', *Temenos II*, London, 1982.

5. Warden, John, *Orpheus: the metamorphosis of a myth*, Toronto, 1982.

6. Warden, J., op. cit.

7. Warden, J., op. cit.

8. What follows here has been deeply influenced by Warden op. cit.

9. Virgil, *Georgics*, Tr. L. P. Wilkinson, London, 1982.

10. Ovid, *Metamorphoses*, Tr. Mary M. Innes, London, 1955 (reprinted).

11. Anon., 'Sir Orfeo', *Gawain and the Green Knight, Pearl, & Sir Orfeo*, London, 1975.

12. Ficino, Marsilio, *Opera Omnia*, 1576 (ed. Sancipriano & Kristeller, Turin, 1962).

13. Mellers, Wilfrid, *Masks of Orpheus*, Manchester, 1987.

14. e.g. Hoban, Russell, *The Medusa Frequency*, London, 1988; Davies, Robertson, *The Lyre of Orpheus*, Canada, 1988.

15. Segal, Charles, *Orpheus, the myth of the poet*, Baltimore, 1989. (Note, his select bibliography includes the following, which give some idea of the recent work on Orpheus: Barkan, Leonard, *The Gods Made Flesh: Metamorphosis and the Pursuit of Paganism*, New Haven, Conn., 1986; Blanchot, Maurice, *The Gaze of Orpheus and Other Literary Essays*, Tr. Lydia Davis, Barrytown, N.Y., 1981; Bowra, C. M., 'Orpheus and Eurydice', *Classical Quarterly*, 1952; Friedman, John B., *Orpheus in the Middle Ages*, Cambridge, Mass., 1970; Graf, Fritz, 'Orpheus: A Poet among Men', in Jan Bremmer ed. *Interpretations of Greek Mythology*, London, 1987; Guthrie, W. K. C., *Orpheus and Greek Religion*, New York, 1952; Lee, M. Owen, 'Orpheus and Eurydice: Some Modern Versions', *Classical Journal*, 1960/61; Lee, M. Owen, 'Orpheus and Eurydice: Myth, Legend, Folklore', *Classica et Mediaevalia*, 1965; Linforth, I. M., *The Arts of Orpheus*, Berkeley & Los Angeles, 1941; Sewell, Elizabeth, *The Orphic Voice: Poetry and Natural History*, New Haven, Conn., 1960; Strauss, Walter A., *Descent and Return: The Orphic Theme in Modern Literature*, Cambridge, Mass., 1971; Warden, John, *Orpheus: The Metamorphosis of a Myth*, Toronto, 1982.

16. Ferrabosco, Alfonso, *Ayres*, London, 1609 (facsimile, Menston, 1970).

17. Ficino, Marsilio, *De Vita Triplici*, Tr. as 'The Book of Life' by Charles Boer, Dallas, 1980.

18. Hawking, Stephen, *A brief history of Time*, London, 1988.

19. Walker, D. P., op. cit.

20. Lovejoy, A. O., *The Great Chain of Being*, Harvard, 1936 (reprinted).

CHAPTER SIX

1. Coprario, John, *Songs of Mourning*, London, 1613 (facsimile, Menston, 1970).

CHAPTER SEVEN

1. Davies, Sir John, 'Nosce teipsum: of human knowledge', *Silver Poets of the 16th century*, (ed.) Gerald Bullett, London, 1947 (reprinted).
2. Warden, John, op. cit.
3. Yates, Frances, *The French Academies of the 16th century*, London, 1947.
4. Rooley, Anthony, 'Patronage', *Compendium of Musical Thought*, York, 1990.

Bibliography

The following brief selection of works includes only those books which have been a real source of inspiration, indeed revelation, over the last twenty-one years. It is a personal, even idiosyncratic, choice of works which have had direct bearing on the development of the spirit of this book. By listing these titles I hope that readers' curiosity in anything I might have written may be turned to the source by which I have been inspired.

Butler, Christopher, *Number Symbolism*, New York, 1970.

Castiglione, B., *The Book of the Courtyer*, Tr. T. Hoby, 1561.

Davies, Stevie, *Renaissance Views of Man*, Manchester, 1979.

Ficino, Marsilio, *The Book of Life*, Tr. C. Boer, Salisbury, 1980.

Fowler, Alastair, *Spenser and the Numbers of Time*, London, 1964.

Freeman, Rosemary, *English Emblem Books*, London, 1948.

French, Peter J., *John Dee: The work of an Elizabethan Magus*, London, 1972.

Gordon, D. J., *The Renaissance Imagination*, (ed.) S. Orgel, London, 1975.

Heniger Jn., S. K., *Touches of Sweet Harmony*, California, 1974.

Ingpen, William, *The secrets of numbers*, London, 1624.

Kristeller, Paul O., *Renaissance Concepts of Man*, New York, 1972.

Lyons, Bridget G., *Voices of Melancholy*, London, 1971.

Parry, Graham, *The Golden Age restor'd*, Manchester, 1985.

Tillyard, E. M. W., *The Elizabethan World Picture*, London, 1968.

Walker, D. P., *Spiritual and Demonic Magic from Ficino to Campanella*, London, 1975.

Warden, John, *Orpheus: the Metamorphosis of a myth*, Toronto, 1982.

Wind, Edgar, *Pagan Mysteries in the Renaissance*, London, 1967.

Yates, Frances, *Astraea: the Imperial Theme in the Sixteenth Century*, London, 1975.

Yates, Frances, *Giordano Bruno and the Hermetic Tradition*, London, 1964.

Yates, Frances, *The Occult in the Elizabethan Age*, London, 1979.

Yates, Frances, *The Rosicrucian Enlightenment*, London, 1972.